Portfolios:

Enriching and Assessing All Students
Identifying the Gifted Grades K-6

Author: **Bertie Kingore** Ph.D.

Illustrator: **Shaula Patton**

First Edition

Text: © Bertie Kingore 199?

© Graphics: Leadership Publishers

Leadership Publishers Inc.
Promoting Leadership & Human Potential
Post Office Box 8358
Des Moines, Iowa 50301

ISBN: 0-911943-33-1

Table of Contents

a

Planned Experiences Using Children's Literature: Copies of Activities

Teacher Resources:

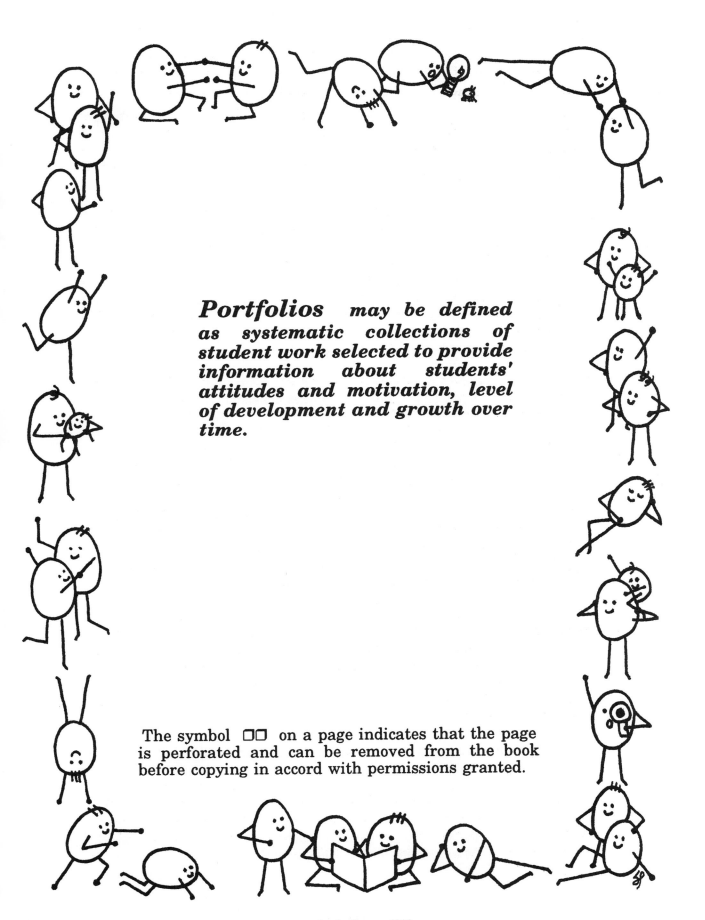

Portfolios may be defined as systematic collections of student work selected to provide information about students' attitudes and motivation, level of development and growth over time.

The symbol ☐☐ on a page indicates that the page is perforated and can be removed from the book before copying in accord with permissions granted.

Introduction

Portfolios may be defined as systematic collections of student work selected to provide information about students' attitudes and motivation, level of development and growth over time.

For many years, assessment of student abilities has centered upon standardized tests, often resulting in the test tail wagging the education dog. Objective tests invite teaching to the test and reward procedures where simple correct answers and memorization are more highly prized than high-level thinking (Worthen & Spandel, 1991).

But to prepare for the future, today's students need to demonstrate abilities to learn and understand material beyond rote facts and basic knowledge. They need education settings which demonstrate that while right answers are valuable, habits of mind and the justification of one's approach and results are at least of equal value (Wiggins, 1990). Thus educators have searched for ways to include a wider range of tasks, materials and use of student abilities while seeking more authentic forms of assessment. Authentic assessment is tasks which are real instances of extended criterion performances, rather than test items estimating learning goals (Lorrie Shepard, interview in Kirst, 1991).

Portfolios are the assessment tool of choice in many professions (Ramsey, 1990). Photographers, artists and writers have always compiled portfolios to showcase their best work. Indeed, most people in today's work force, while not formally developing portfolios, are nonetheless assessed on actual job performance and most certainly not multiple-choice tests. In education settings, however, many adults have believed that standardized tests are necessary as the only way to ensure objectivity, fairness and consistency in student (or school) assessment. Portfolio assessment is not standardized, but that fact should not imply that it is without standards. Portfolio assessment strives to establish standards without standardization by enabling educators to assess student products against specific criteria (Wiggins, 1990). In reality, the debate is not whether to rely on standardized tests or product portfolios, but rather how to employ both to provide more accurate and complete profiles of the needs and abilities of learners.

The use of student products as part of the assessment of students is not a revolutionary idea. Programs have always graded some physical products produced by students as one aspect of the students' growth and ability. In most cases, however, such grades were determined by a single teacher. Inasmuch as different educators invariably used different criteria in assigning grades to such products, inconsistencies emerged and made the use of products a less reliable measure of assessment.

Many dedicated teachers have even tried to keep "work folders" for each student in a certain subject. While these work folders proved very effective for some teachers, they frustrated other teachers who were often unsure how to best organize the process, what specifically to include in the folders, and how to determine the value of what they had collected. Some collections eventually ended up more sporadic than originally intended as teachers did not have the time to organize the folders and file the students' work.

A portfolio must be much more than just some "stuff" students produce and teachers save. Product portfolios involve a systemic and organized collection of student materials consistently used by most or all teachers and students across curriculum content areas and across the school district to validate growth and abilities. Shirley Frye, past president of the National Council of Teachers of Mathematics, considers a portfolio a showcase of student work that focuses on growth over time. The contents of a portfolio should reveal the changes and consistencies of each student's attitudes and thinking processes, provide evidence of areas of achievement and success for the learner, and serve as a basis for discussion among the student, teacher and parent (Stenmark, 1991).

Portfolios offer promise as both a means for enriching all students through an authentic assessment of ability and growth, and simultaneously for identifying gifted students. Portfolios may be defined as systematic collections of student work selected to provide information about students' attitudes and motivation, level of development and growth over time. Portfolios allow a more complex and comprehensive view of student performance which encourages educators to consider the complex and multidimensional process of learning. (Paulson & Paulson, 1990).

In order for portfolios to be educationally effective, then, some key words and phrases emerge. Portfolios must emphasize product, process, and content, effort and achievement, student ownership, and self-evaluation. Portfolios must be developed so they:

- *are a natural part of daily classroom activities rather than contrived;*

- *are thoroughly integrated into the instructional program;*

- *encourage student responsibility, ownership and pride of accomplishment;*

- *allow students to polish and refine their craft - to build upon what they are learning to do well;*

- *focus discussions about learning and development among students, teachers and parents;*

- *incorporate learning tasks and also students' ideas, interests and attitudes;*

- *invite challenge and complexity in students' thinking and in the works they produce;*

- *encourage student metacognition and increase their awareness of their capacity for self-reflection and making judgments.*

Portfolios: Enriching All Students, Identifying the Gifted presents the organization, procedures, values and evaluation of product portfolios for all students while providing additional materials and procedures to assist in the identification of potentially gifted students. While portfolios are applicable to any age group, this book describes the use of portfolios with kindergarten through sixth grade students. The procedures discussed in this book are being used nationally by numerous districts to encourage and assess all students while identifying gifted students.

Background

> The debate is not whether to rely on standardized tests *or* portfolios, but rather how to employ both to provide more accurate and complete profiles of the needs and abilities of learners.

In 1971, U.S. Commissioner of Education Sidney Marland warned that exclusive reliance on intelligence and achievement tests, grades, and teacher recommendation for identification of the gifted would eliminate half of our gifted and talented youth from consideration for programs for the gifted. Ten years after the Marland report, the National Report on Identification (Richert, Alvino, & McDonnell, 1982) noted that there was still heavy reliance on such instruments for the identification of the gifted at both the nomination and assessment stages, and that minority gifted remained grossly under-represented in programs for the gifted throughout the nation. The inability of gifted ethnic minority students to conquer the twin hurdles of achievement and intelligence tests is cited as one of the major causes of under-representation of these students in gifted programs (Bernal, 1978; Ford & Harris, 1990; Richert, 1987).

Exclusive reliance on intelligence and achievement tests is also counterproductive with our young elementary students. The scores of young children on intelligence tests have been shown to be less reliable than those of older children in predicting later scores on these tests (Karnes, 1987; Marland, 1971; Roedell, Jackson & Robinson, 1980). Certainly achievement test scores for children encountering academics for the first time are inappropriate criteria for identifying young gifted children. Most school districts have solved these problems of lack of predictability and of applicability of standardized measurements in the identification of the young gifted by declining to identify or provide programs for these students (Karnes, 1987; Kitano & Kirby, 1986).

Clearly, alternatives to identification through standardized testing should be a priority for teachers of elementary-aged students. As one example of alternative identification procedures, the National Report on Identification (Richert et.al., 1982) called for the development of product evaluations to aid in the identification of gifted children.

Simultaneously, regular education programs, searching for alternatives to achievement testing for all students, are also exploring product evaluation. The Association for Supervision and Curriculum Development (ASCD) identified portfolios as one of the top three curriculum trends, thus indicating that administrators, policy makers and teachers are investigating new standards for student performance (Vavrus, 1990).   Portfolios of student products are currently receiving increased attention as an assessment alternative in such content areas as reading, writing, and math (Costa, 1989; Mills, 1989, Wolf, 1989) and in multiple state programs such as those in California, Michigan, Illinois, Rhode Island and Texas (Chapman, 1990; Maeroff, 1991).

One of the most ambitious portfolio projects was initiated in 1990 in Vermont, where the first statewide assessment to combine product portfolios and standardized tests has begun to measure a broader gauge of student knowledge and skills than traditional tests alone provide. Vermont will assess the writing and mathematics achievement of fourth and eighth grade students through a standardized test, a portfolio of each student's significant products in those two curriculum areas, and a "best piece" where students select from their portfolios the works that represent their best effort for the year.   The purpose of the statewide assessment is not to compare students but rather to learn how well Vermont students write and apply math skills.   The goal is to expand portfolios into additional grade levels and other areas of the curriculum over the next few years (Vermont, 1990).

Richard P. Mills, Vermont's Commissioner of Education, stated, "We are undertaking this massive project because we are interested in *real* student work, *real* performance, not the proxy delivered by standardized, short-answer tests"(1989, p.11). Through specific teacher-student interaction and communication, portfolios could help encourage educators and students to work together to increase student achievement.   Mills noted, "This is a vast conspiracy to boost the performance of every single child in Vermont.   What we're looking at is not high test scores, but great schools" (Rothman, 1990, p.1).

Thus, portfolios of student products provide exciting promise for districts dissatisfied with more traditional assessment procedures. Portfolios also offer promise as a non-traditional alternative to standardized testing for the identification of gifted students.   Because every student develops a portfolio for assessment, this identification method offers opportunities for ethnic minority, impoverished, handicapped and young gifted students to demonstrate abilities that might not be revealed through standardized testing.

Development and Field Testing

This portfolio project began as the author worked with several districts interested in incorporating indicators of student achievement beyond just standardized test results. One objective was to investigate the structure, contents, process, values, and evaluation of student portfolios so that districts might successfully implement portfolios with maximum value for all students without overburdening teachers with the clerical details involved in the collection and assessment of products for the portfolio. A second objective was to investigate the use of portfolios as one criterion in the identification of gifted children.

The results, as explained in this book, developed over a three year period as hundreds of kindergarten through sixth grade teachers implemented portfolios with the students in their classrooms. The procedures and activities were initially field tested in a small number of classrooms. Those results were analyzed for their effectiveness and revisions implemented in response to administrators' and teachers' feedback and suggestions. The procedures and activities were then implemented in a large number of classrooms with the results undergoing further analysis and revision. White, Asian, Black, Hispanic and Native American students whose socioeconomic status ranged from poverty level through upper-middle class were involved in the project. The school districts included both rural and urban districts ranging in size from approximately 200 to 60,000 students per district.

A special thank you and warm regards to the hundreds of teachers and thousands of students in Colorado, Georgia, Illinois, Iowa, Michigan, Ohio, Oregon and Texas whose cooperation, suggestions, questions, feedback, and candor were invaluable in helping implement and refine this process.

Examples of student's works and completed sample forms throughout this publication are based on composites or replicas of actual student or district products. Exact names and/or examples are not used to protect the anonymity of each student.

Limitations

1. Portfolios need district-wide or at least school-wide implementation and standards to achieve the greatest value, effect, and consistency.

2. Portfolio assessment requires administrators and teachers who believe in its value and are well trained in its implementation.

3. Portfolios and authentic assessment cannot succeed without ongoing teacher inservice. Teachers and administrators must not only understand the assessment, but also adapt their objectives and instructional methods to guide students throughout the process.

4. Portfolios and authentic assessment must evolve over a prolonged period of time. Educators cannot successfully change to this student-centered assessment, which intersects instruction and evaluation, without ample time for implementation and refinement.

5. As with any assessment or identification measure, the effectiveness of portfolios requires that they be carefully planned, well organized, and conscientiously implemented. If a portfolio is to be of any diagnostic or assessment value to students, parents, and educators it must be more than "just some stuff" someone puts in a folder. It must be more than a random collection of grade-level workbook pages.

6. Portfolio assessment is valid only if the <u>process</u> of producing those products is also observed and understood. To avoid leaping to conclusions, educators must analyze products in the context of the assigned task.

7. To maximize the value and effectiveness of portfolios, educators must be willing to practice the same levels of higher order thinking expected of students. We must:

   <u>Analyze</u> what students are trying to do;

   <u>Synthesize</u> data from products and observations about each student to determine significant patterns of strengths and needs;

   <u>Evaluate</u> the instructional needs of each student based upon our analysis and synthesis over a period of time.

8. While all students can successfully do some higher order thinking activities designed for the gifted, if all students are equally completing all the activities, then the gifted are not being sufficiently challenged.

9. The activities and procedures suggested in this publication do not constitute or substitute for a differentiated gifted curriculum. These are only seeds which encourage the screening of <u>all</u> children for gifted potentials.

10. In order to validate the effectiveness of portfolios in the process of gifted identification, further data are being collected to substantiate the idea that products indeed predict success in gifted programs. Correlations of the portfolio data with the criteria of success in the program will indicate if there is accurate identification. Districts are encouraged to research such correlations within their own programs and to increase their awareness of examples of specific tasks and products which prove particularly helpful in screening for gifted students in their populations.

Portfolios:
Enriching All Students

Portfolio: Enriching All Students

Authentic Assessment

Product portfolios integrate with authentic assessment because they represent actual learning experiences occurring for all students in elementary classrooms. They have the potential to validate student growth over a period of time through a sampling of real student works rather than the proxy represented on standardized tests (Mills, 1989). To use portfolios to their maximum potential, educators must determine the structure of the portfolios, how items are to be selected for inclusion, the values and uses for the portfolios and the evaluation of portfolio products.

Conceptual Structure

Vavrus (1990) notes that effective portfolios have both a physical structure and a less obvious but vital conceptual structure. The conceptual structure is the planning and decision-making behind a portfolio project which establishes the priorities and long-term value of the process. As a district attempts to initiate portfolio assessment, it must first make decisions about its concept of portfolios (Mill, 1989; Rothman, 1990; Vavrus, 1990). Such decisions about conceptual structure are based upon a clarification and communication of multiple factors including, but not limited to, the questions posed on the checklist for Conceptual Structure (next page).

Conceptual Structure of Portfolios: Checklist

1. How will portfolios integrate with school, district and/or state goals?

2. What are our underlying goals for portfolio assessment?
   Do we intend portfolios to:

   _____ Collaborate evidence suggested by test scores;

   _____ Document behaviors that tests can not measure;

   _____ Substantiate outcomes;

   _____ Increase effectiveness of instruction;

   _____ Increase students' responsibility and organizational skills;

   _____ Increase the effectiveness of teacher, student and parent communication regarding achievement;

   _____ Replace grades or grade cards;

   _____ Other _____

3. What are our long-term goals for portfolios? What do we hope to have accomplished after five years of implementation of this project?

4. Upon which learning objectives for students do we wish portfolios to focus?

   Curriculum content areas(s):

   Outcomes:

   Specific skill development priorities:

   Critical and productive thinking skill priorities:

5. What types of selected student products might best document the designated learning objectives?

   ___Written Products ___ Audiotapes ___Videotapes ___Graphics ___Computer-generated products

   Other _____

6. Will the portfolio contain only the best work of students, reflect their learning growth and progress over time, or both?

7. Who is the intended audience for these products?

   ___ Students-teacher conferences ___ Parents ___ Peers ___ Other teachers

   _____ Administrators   _____ District or state assessment teams

   Other _____

8. What will each of these audiences want to know about student learning and assessment?

9. Which forms of communication might best assist the implementation of portfolio assessment?

   _____ Teacher inservice   _____ Written materials _____ School-based portfolio teams

   _____ Parent meetings and letters   _____ Networking with other schools/districts

   Other_____

Physical Structure and Storage

The physical structure refers to the format and organization of the actual products used to demonstrate student progress. For example, portfolio products may be arranged chronologically, may represent a single content area or be divided into several different subject areas, or may even be arranged according to categories or styles of work such as graphics, problem solving and skill development.

The physical structure also refers to the container which stores the portfolio products. The significance of portfolios is determined by what is in the container rather than the container itself. In classrooms across the nation, a wide variety of containers is being used for portfolios, including plastic bins, boxes, shopping bags, and expandable folders of every shape and kind. The decision regarding which container to use depends upon four factors. The container needs to:

1. Be strong enough to withstand a whole year's use;
2. Occupy no more classroom space than is comfortably available in most classrooms;
3. Be economically feasible;
4. Be readily accessible to students so the portfolios can be a natural part of daily classroom activities.

Because of these four factors, the portfolio itself is most often a standard file folder for each student, stored in a filing cabinet drawer readily accessible to students. For more personalization, each student designs his/her portfolio at the beginning of the year. After the designing is complete, some teachers choose to laminate each student's portfolio folder to increase its durability throughout the year. These designed portfolios become a product in themselves.

Throughout the year, the students put their name and the date on each product and file it in their portfolio - consistently in the front or back of each folder to keep their products in a chronological sequence. Many teachers prefer that the students file new products in the back of the folder. Thus, each time a product is added, the student sees his/her earlier work and is reminded of how much has been learned and how much progress has been achieved. Even the children in kindergarten and first grades can successfully get some representation of their name and date on each paper. Dating items is especially important as it will help establish the developmental progression of each child over time. To help young children successfully date their work, some teachers simply write the numerals for the date on the chalkboard and children copy them on their paper as needed. Other teachers purchase a date stamp with rotating numeral tracks, and let children stamp the date on each product.

During field testing, one first grade teacher did not want to put the names of her children on their portfolio folders. She feared that the children would become too concerned about what each was doing and would be negatively comparing themselves all the time. She decided to use the art design for each portfolio to identify it instead of using students' names. After a couple of weeks, the teacher was attempting to put some products in the portfolios and was having difficulty remembering whose was whose. As she pondered over one portfolio, one of her first graders noticed her problem and said, *"Oh, that's Anita's portfolio. You want Louisa's - the one with the cat on it."* At that, another child added, *"You've going the wrong way. Look right in front of Matt's with the army tanks on it."* The teacher realized she was the only one in the room who could not identify the owner of each portfolio! All the children were aware of and yet not particularly bothered by the differences in what others were or were not doing because they were in a classroom where everyone was made to feel valued and important. They were learning, through the teacher's warmth and modeling, that they were not all the same; they were individuals and each was very important. Subsequently the teacher put the children's names on their folders so she wouldn't be the only one having difficulty identifying portfolios.

It is very important that the physical structure of the portfolios allow the majority of the filing, organization and management to be completed by the students themselves. Teachers do not need additional paperwork, and students increase their ownership in the portfolio and benefit from the responsibility as they assume most of the portfolio management duties. As they file their work, students become increasingly aware of their own progress and are heard to make comments such as, *"I'm sure working harder,"* and *"Oh, that was a good story; but this one has much better character development."* Thus, portfolios can be motivating and intrinsically rewarding to students as the portfolio process allows students to become their own advocate through self-selection of their work.

Product Collection

Since portfolios represent real learning activities ongoing in classrooms, it follows that one must select work samples indicative of a wide variety of curriculum areas and assignments in which students are engaged. Wiggins advises that authentic assessments must "present the student with the full array of tasks that mirror the priorities and challenges found in the best instructional activities," such as conducting research, revising, and collaborating, and must allow opportunities to "craft polish" (1990,3). For a greater value and more complete assessment, two categories of student products are collected for student portfolio:

- collected work samples, and

  •• spontaneous products.

Initially, the objective is to collect a range of works, deliberately diverse, which later can be refined to a small body of finished work.

• Collected Work Samples

Collected work samples are the basic foundation of the entire portfolio. Periodically, each student selects and dates significant products in specific curriculum areas such as writing, science, math, social studies, and reading. Obviously, not every piece of work would be included in the portfolio, but the portfolio should be complete enough to reflect the ongoing curriculum at each grade level (Vermont, 1990). For example, if one sample in three curriculum areas was collected every three weeks, a student would have accumulated approximately 30-40 products in his/her portfolio by the end of the year. This quantity of student work proves extremely useful to the student, teacher and parent in validating learning and assessing student performance and growth in each content area throughout the year.

Collected works must be more than grade-bound worksheets if educators desire product excellence and evidence of higher order thinking and problem solving from all students (Hagen, 1980; Long & Clemmons, 1982; Paulson, Paulson & Meyer, 1990). One district administrator called our project office to request assistance because their portfolios were not substantiating any high-level responses from students. A review of the portfolios revealed a collection of pages from grade level reading and math workbooks, and handwriting practice pages of material carefully copied from the chalkboard. Believing that these product choices allowed little opportunity for outstanding performance, we encouraged the district to restructure its curriculum to increase higher level thinking and to set up more opportunities to elicit problem solving abilities and originality. As Hagen admonished in Identification of the Gifted, "If the tasks set by the teacher never, or seldom, require high-level, problem-solving abilities or originality, then the teacher will not be able to observe whether an individual has these abilities" (1980, p.12).

The instructional tasks and problems valued for portfolio collection are those which are integrated, complex and challenging. They must require students to analyze and synthesize to arrive at explanations or solutions. Thus for maximum assessment potential for all students and application to the identification of gifted students, the collected work should include more open-ended products designed to elicit higher-level thinking and allow grade-level and even above grade-level work. The products should also be

14

more than just finished pieces. Indeed, first drafts as well as finished work can serve to evaluate growth and reflect multiple stages of student thinking and product development. Ideas, sketches and revisions will at times add insight regarding a student's learning process and growth. Many teachers had a rubber stamp made which said "draft". Then students could stamp their first drafts or ideas and works in progress so others would know what each edition was. In addition, collected work samples should include computer products and non-written products such as audiotapes, to broaden the range of materials used beyond paper and pencil tasks. Audiotapes, for example, can validate the fluency and vocabulary growth in students' oral reading (see Reading Tape Form, page 19). Audiotapes are also a useful tool with pre-readers or non-readers to convey their thinking, depth of content understanding and problem solving ability. Every student should have approximately the same number of collected work samples in his/her portfolio.

• • Spontaneous Products

Spontaneous products are products which develop unexpectedly in the course of daily school work or may be brought in by the student from home. Occasionally one or more students will produce something unexpected which is of particular instructional interest. These products may indicate a level of excellence that is characteristic of an advanced or gifted child or, quite the opposite, may indicate students needing special help.

Every student will not have the same number or kind of spontaneous products in his/her portfolio. Spontaneous products will vary in quantity for each student because some students will more frequently and consistently produce products which differ from those typical for that grade level. Some students will bring in more products produced out of school. Spontaneous products will also vary in quality for each student as some students produce outstanding class work in areas where other students may be struggling. Indeed, students who produce only grade-level expected products and never bring to school a product completed at home may actually have no spontaneous products in their portfolio.

Unexpected products have always developed in classrooms and caused teachers delight as they enjoy the student's success or thoughtful concern as they analyze long-term ramifications regarding the needs of the student. Clearly no single product can be conclusive regarding the needs of a student. By collecting both spontaneous products and work samples over a period of time, a teacher may establish patterns of students' abilities and collect physical evidence to validate the desirability of additional sources of information or testing for a student with needs beyond the regular classroom at either end of the ability continuum.

Thus collected work samples and spontaneous products work together and prove important and useful for all students. Because of the portfolios, these products are readily available throughout the year as instructional decisions need to be made or substantiated.

Examples of Products to Collect

Attention to real, meaningful tasks is a crucial consideration in selecting products. A portfolio should largely reflect an integral part of the curriculum, rather than artificial activities and isolated skills. Portfolio items might include any of the following. This list is not inclusive of every possible kind of work which could be selected. Rather, it is meant to provide ideas of the wide range of possible products.

- *Art (natural/creative explorations instead of 'crafts') which shows perspective, objects with two- or three-dimensional figures, texture, form and/or unusual or mature viewpoint.*

- *Photographs of three dimensional products such as math manipulations, math patterns with concrete objects, sculptures, models, dioramas, or block constructions.*

- *Photocopies of awards or honors earned by a student which help understand the whole student and reveal her/his interests.*

- *Language experience dictations, originally written reports, math story problems, stories, literature extensions, poems or plays.*

- *Written and/or student-dictated tapes of problem-solving ideas, inventions, experiments, and/or plans for organizing instructional data for some content area.*

- *First drafts and revised writing should be included, but with a note attached or 'draft' stamp clarifying which edition it is.*

- *Math samples which evidence higher level thinking, such as analysis of problem situations or processes, problem solutions, graphs, patterns, charts, statistical studies and survey results.*

- *Charts, graphs, and webbing or mind mapping activities completed by a student which reflect depth of content learned.*

- A student's written or audiotaped personal response to an event, issue, problem or news media story.

- Connections of subject area concepts or skills to real world situations or to other subject areas. See "Reading Review Form" page 18.

- Reading logs, writing logs, math logs, and/or science logs reflecting quantity of work in specific content areas.

- Sample list of trade book titles read and reviewed by student which reveals reading complexity and topics of interest to student. These book lists help document student attitudes toward reading.

- Photocopy or original page from journal entries are an excellent way to include first-draft writing inasmuch as they are typically not graded or rewritten.

- Lab reports documenting a student's analysis and interpretation of results from a scientific observation or experiment.

- Self-evaluations and reflections.

- A videotape of a student or small group presenting information or research results in content areas such as math, science or social studies.

- Audiotapes of students' oral reading. See "Reading Tape Form" page 19.

- Computer-generated examples of student work.

- Group reports or projects; the names of all group members should be listed or at least an indication attached noting that it was group work.

- Collections which relate to topics within content areas.

_____'s READING REVIEW

Date	Title & Author of Book	Rating	This book is important to me because:

_____'s Reading Tape

Tape#	Date	Title	Student Choice	Teacher Choice

Selection of Portfolio Products

The product selection process can incorporate a collaborative interaction between teacher and student. However, if portfolios are viewed as tools for student empowerment in their own learning, then students must maintain the major responsibility for choosing portfolio products. As students engage in product selection for their portfolios, they increase their awareness of their own strengths and abilities. The selection process encourages them to assume greater responsibility for their own learning, and to increase their pride of accomplishment in the portfolio contents. Students should have freedom to choose what they put in their portfolios but they should learn to think carefully about their choices and to share a reason for their selection.

Product selection needs to be made after students review and analyze several of their products. Maximum self-evaluation and reflection occur when students save products for several days and then review all the products before selecting one to place in their portfolio. Completed products may be stored by the student in a folder until time to make a product selection.

Some students easily managed this holding folder/working folder/storage folder (teacher coined several names for this folder) by keeping it in their desks. For other students, however, the holding folders were best stored in a central location in the room. In the latter case, teachers typically provided a portable cardboard file, hanging file or box to store these folders. The completed work, graded or ungraded, is filed by the student in his or her holding folder. Then, at designated times, students review their work, analyze its merits according to classroom established criteria, and make a selection of one product to place in their portfolios. The unselected works may then be taken home. Thus, parents periodically received sets of completed school work.

While students have the most important role in the selection and assessment of their work, they need guidance in establishing criteria for selecting products for their portfolios. Initial classroom experiences with students selecting portfolio products verified to teachers that students, especially the younger ones, do not always understand how to choose what constitutes their best or most significant work. For example, several teachers of kindergarten through second grade reported that their children often choose for their portfolios spelling papers or simple pictures, sometimes even duplicated sheets, which they have colored or completed neatly. Their criteria for selection ranged from *"I got them all right,"* to *"It's pretty,"* to *"I never went outside the lines even once!"* Teachers in grade three through six also initially repeated that students most frequently chose work which was totally correct or had a high grade on it. Their major criteria for selection was neatness, degree of perfection, and grade. These students had learned from significant adults earlier in their learning careers that simple correct answers and being neat and error-free were the most important and desirable goals. While these factors may be a part of assessment, they are not the only criteria students should think about when involved in self-evaluation. These examples illustrate that students need discussion with teachers and other students which focus on a variety of criteria for selecting products. We can not expect students to do something well if they have never been taught to do it. Most students have had little experience in personally evaluating their learning.

Thus teachers realize the importance of teaching children how to establish significant criteria for product selection. Class discussions of possible criteria and charts of criteria ideas help model the decision-making processes of product selection to the children. The teacher can guide the students' establishment of criteria by discussing together key questions such as:

* *What really makes something your best work?*

* *What examples do you want to keep in your portfolio to represent what you are learning throughout the year?*

* *How is this product different from other pieces of your work?*

* *How does this product show something important that you think or feel?*

* *How does this product show something important that that you have learned?*

These questions would not be addressed in one sitting. Rather, a teacher might focus on one question at a time and gradually build student understanding. For example, the following conversation illustrates one discussion in a fourth grade class regarding how to determine best work.

Teacher:	I want you to think carefully about what products you will choose for your portfolio. You may want the products to be your best work. But what really makes something your best work?
Terrance:	It's something you got a good grade on.
Teacher:	All right. What's another idea?
Erin:	It's something you did without any mistakes.
Teacher:	Okay. Now let's stretch our thinking some more. Could your work ever be correctly done, all right, and <u>not</u> be your best work?
Cynthia:	Yeah! If it was too easy it could be all right and not be your best.

Brian:	Yeah, like if you were doing first grade math problems or something. That's too easy to be your best.
Teacher:	And what about making mistakes? Could you ever have mistakes in your work and it still be your best work?
Ruth:	Well, (pause) I don't think so.
J.P.:	Maybe . . . like you were trying something new - something really hard - then you would make mistakes because it was so hard. But it could still be your best. You could be proud of yourself for trying something so hard.

Self-evaluation or reflecting upon what has been accomplished is initially a difficult task for most students. Over time, such discussions help students grow in their ability to self-evaluate.

The captions of one second grade, for example, began in September with comments such as: *"This is good. I like it."* By February, the student's captions reflected an increased level of analysis.

I choose this ___lab report___ for my portfolio because ___I used more science words than I use to know and my observations show good thinking.___

A class might also work together to develop a simple chart of criteria for individuals to view and informally review when selecting portfolio products. This chart would best be an ongoing list of criteria worded in the vocabulary expressed by the students as the key questions on page 21 are discussed. The following is a chart of criteria that emerged from discussion in one class.

Criteria Chart: Third Grade Classroom

> **I can select for my portfolio:**
> * Something that shows or tells what I think
> * My best work so far in _____
> * Something important I've learned
> * A hard problem I figured out
> * Some work that shows how much I've progressed in _____
> * Something complex that shows my thinking
> * A picture that shows what I feel

As students reflect on criteria such as these, they develop their ability to monitor and evaluate their own progress (Vavrus, 1990). They become increasingly sensitive to quality and learn to more objectively and accurately recognize a broader range of criteria in their work. Because student insights are valued in the selection of their portfolio products, their responsibility for learning grows (Vavrus, 1990) and their pride of accomplishment increases.

One objective of the portfolio process is to showcase and encourage the best work of each student. Many students are more motivated to try to excel and do their best when they select the products which become a part of their portfolio. Students learn to choose products which best represent their abilities, interests and accomplishments so their portfolio can reflect who they are when they aren't available to represent themselves to another.

As one example of managing this selection process, on Monday the teacher may announce to the class that they will each be reviewing the last few weeks of their work in writing to select their best written product for their portfolios. *"On Friday, I will remind you to review your writing for the past three weeks to select a piece for your portfolio."* To avoid the problem of the entire class lining up to file their choices, most teachers find it productive to suggest a time span during which students could take turns filing. *"When you have made your choice, write a caption to attach to your product and then file it in your portfolio any time when there is room at the filing drawer between now and lunch."*

Occasionally, teachers might also select items to go in the portfolios. Teacher-selected products represent student work which is of particular instructional interest to the teacher. The teacher would announce to the class as they begin the assignment that this assignment will be added to their portfolios. For example, after completing an extensive and long-term investigation on a topic, the teacher might use a mind-map or webbing activity as a culminating experience to substantiate what each individual has learned. *"Design and complete a mind map to show your best thinking regarding what you have learned about electricity. Your map will be one item placed in your portfolio this week."*

Captions: Students' Reflective Thinking

One major goal of portfolios is metacognitive -- to involve students in self assessment and help them develop the ability to reflect and make judgments about their work according to established criteria (Flood and Lapp, 1989; Paulson & Paulson, 1990; Tierney, Carter & Desai, 1991). Educators and parents find they gain insights into the thinking and motivation of each child by having children attach a brief note of explanation to each product placed in their portfolio. Called captioning, this process simply has students write or dictate personalized statements sharing why they choose that specific product. This reflection can focus on a discussion of strengths and needs using a simple scoring system devised by the district or using a series of questions which invite student responses. The form with which most teachers had greatest success was open-ended sentences, such as the examples that follow. A student typically completed one of the sentence prompts in her/his own words and stapled it to a product before filing the product in the portfolio.

Sample captions:

* *"I choose this _____ for my portfolio because ..."*

* *"I think this _____ is my best work because ..."*

* *"This product shows ...."*

* *"I want this _____ in my portfolio because ...."*

* *"I think I did better work on this _____ by ..."*

* *"This assignment was easy (hard) for me because..."*

Students selecting their best work and captioning to explain their choices allows students to become their own advocates. They are empowered to help others understand their thinking and their priorities in learning.

As an alternative, caption or product labels like the one that follows could be duplicated and provided to the students.

Product Label

Date _____

Name _____

School _____

Grade _____ Teacher _____

_____ *Student Selected*   _____ *Teacher Selected*

I think I did better work on this _____

_____

by _____

_____

(completed sample) # Product Label

Date ___ *November 4, 1991*

Name *Jeff Williams*

School *Bryant Elementary*

Grade *fourth* Teacher ___ *Ms. Wihert*

_____ *Student Selected*   _____ *Teacher Selected*

I think I did better work on this ___ *report on*

Benjamin Franklin's later years

by *comparing him to modern inventors* _____ .
instead of just copying from the encyclopiedia.

The label on the previous page is an interesting and thoughtful reflection. It verifies the type of self-evaluative thinking that captions can prompt.

Some students, however, viewed these duplicated labels as busy work - especially if they had to fill in the same information everytime on the label, e.g., school, grade and teacher's name. After more experience, many teachers concluded that, in regard to the management of portfolios, the simpler the better. By listing open-ended sentences for captions on a chart and displaying it clearly in the room, students could copy and complete a caption as they needed one and the teacher did not have to duplicate or cut apart anything. Teachers even used the captions as handwriting practice for students. Students could practice letter formations by writing the open-ended caption statements which contain the alphabet letters being taught, and thus supply themselves with a set of caption strips ready to complete as needed. This incorporation of handwriting practice and caption strips proved especially helpful for primary grade students. They prepared caption strips at one time and filled in the blanks at another time, thus reducing the writing task at any one sitting.

End of Year Reflections

Inasmuch as a major instructional goal of portfolios is metacognition, many experiences have been provided during the portfolio process to help students increase their ability to self-reflect. The portfolio process has encouraged the student to form criteria, assess work according to those criteria, celebrate when meeting the expectations implied in those criteria, and determine goals for continued growth. This is an empowering process which increases students' responsibility in their own learning.

At the end of the year, students can reflect on the growth evidenced by the entire portfolio. Students review their collections and write or dictate their reflection of what has changed with time, what is characteristic, what needs to be done and how they feel about their portfolio (Wolf, 1989). Teachers called these responses reflections or reflective letters and they became a final product in the portfolio.

Katie, for example, reviewed all of her portfolio in May of first grade and dictated the following reflection to her teacher.

"I really learned a lot. I can use words to make you know what I think about. I like to write math stories and people stories. My mommi will be so proud of this."

Daniel, an eighth grader, wrote this concluding paragraph in his reflective letter reacting to his total portfolio in English.

"With this wide range of content and organization, I respectfully request your application for the sincerity of my efforts. I am very proud of these compositions and the writing growth I demonstrated this year."

It is interesting that the conclusions of both Katie and Daniel are so similar in focus. Both accent pride as a key concept of their response to their total portfolio. The portfolio process enabled students to take pride in what they had accomplished. This pride is a viable reason for initiating and continuing the portfolio process.

Parent Communication

Communication between the home and the school is an important part of the portfolio process. As the Dutch adage states: *"What you're not up on, you're down on!"* Thus, parents need to be aware of the objectives and process of the project so they will understand when their child talks about his/her portfolio. Furthermore, informed parents can help their child choose some products from home to take to school; many children complete work at home that would add insights into the whole child if that work could be included in the child's portfolio. In this manner, parental involvement in the assessment process is encouraged and parents increase their awareness of the abilities of their children.

Information about the portfolios may be shared in classroom meetings for groups of parents, PTA meetings and/or parent conferences. But letters to parents are another communication source which effectively informs the parents of the project. It is vital, of course, that all parent information and letters are available in the home language of the student.

Letters to parents should provide general information about portfolios for their child and should also help parents collect samples of their child's work completed away from school. Two sample letters and a page of caption strips are included here to model this communication link. Additional parent letters and a parent response form are included in the discussion of conferencing with portfolios (see pages 46, 47.)

Initially, teachers reported that few parents responded or sent products from home. But as the year progressed, parents' interest and active involvement often increased as the children became increasingly involved in their own portfolios. Furthermore, teachers noted that during conferences parents were very interested in viewing and discussing their child's portfolio even if it did not contain any products from home.

On the next pages are two sample letters to parents:
1. Introducing the Portfolio Process;
2. Captions on Products from Home.

28

Date _____

Dear Parent(s):

The products children produce throughout the school year help us gain a better understanding of children's needs, interests and progress. The actual work that children complete over time provides a richer and more authentic way than tests alone to assess what they are learning and the depth of their thinking.

Thus, all year, we will be collecting and storing many of your child's products in these curriculum areas (list curriculum areas):

_____.

This collection is called a <u>portfolio</u> and will contain first drafts as well as refined pieces to better show how your child thinks, works and how much your child is learning. This portfolio will be largely managed by the children to develop their organization skills and extend their responsibility and ownership in their work. Children will be encouraged to produce their best work and select products for their portfolio which show how capable they are.

When children select a product to go in their portfolios, we ask them to think about the following questions:

* *What really makes something your best work?*

* *What examples do you want to keep in your portfolio to represent what you are learning throughout the year?*

* *How is this product different from other pieces of your work?*

* *How does this product show something important that you think or feel?*

* *How does this product show something important that you have learned?*

The children will keep their work at school for several days before they review it to select a product for their portfolio. The products not selected for their portfolio will be sent home in a packet (state schedule for sending products home) _____.

Children may also produce some things at home that show their talents. Throughout the year, please encourage your child to bring a few examples from home to include in his/her portfolio. At the end of the year, this most exciting portfolio collection will be shared with you to show the growth your child makes this year.

Sincerely,

_____
(signature: teacher or administrator)

Date _____

Dear Parent(s),

Each child has designed his/her portfolio and we are beginning to collect a few portfolio products. We ask your help in identifying your child's special interests and talents. When your child completes a product at home that shows a hobby or interest or is especially well done, please send that product to school to go in his/her portfolio. You may send a photograph of the product if it is a three-dimensional item such as a model or sculpture. Other examples may include:

* collections

* tape recordings of stories, drama or musical productions

* drawings, paintings, or photographs of sculptures

* original math ideas, problems or graphs

* a letter written by your child which expresses
    his/her ideas or opinions

* problem solving examples

* photocopies of awards

It is very important to your child's self-esteem that you send products completed only by your child. We want children to feel proud of their work because they have tried hard to do their best. When others do work for children it is harder for children to feel proud and confident. From time to time, praise your child's efforts and help your child select an example of what he/she has done well to include in the portfolio at school.

Please always be sure your child's name and the date are written on the back of the product. We also ask you to complete with your child a brief note to attach to each product. Just cut off one of the caption strips on the next page and write as many of your child's own words as possible to help us better understand your child's thinking.

Sincerely,

_____
(signature: teacher)

I chose this ___math story problem___ for my portfolio
because ___it is the hardest one I have ever made up.___
___It uses multiplication and subtraction. I worked___
___a long time to do it ._____.

---✂--✂--✂--✂--✂--✂--✂--✂--✂--✂--✂--✂--✂--✂--✂--✂--✂--✂

I chose this _____for my portfolio

because _____

_____

_____.

---✂--✂--✂--✂--✂--✂--✂--✂--✂--✂--✂--✂--✂--✂--✂--✂--✂--✂

I chose this _____for my portfolio

because _____

_____

_____.

---✂--✂--✂--✂--✂--✂--✂--✂--✂--✂--✂--✂--✂--✂--✂--✂--✂--✂

I chose this _____for my portfolio

because _____

_____

_____.

Value of Portfolios for All Students

Standardized test scores are routinely used to evaluate students and programs. In a standardized test, specific questions are asked, answers are given, and the result is a score. But such a process typically does not evaluate the student's level of thinking and problem solving. A standard score does not reflect how students sometimes get the wrong answer for the right reasons, as when their thinking is more complex and divergent than the simple, literal answer intended. A portfolio system presents a kind of assessment tool that goes beyond the one-dimensional scores of multiple-choice tests.

Portfolios offer many advantages over traditional forms of assessment of student abilities and achievements. As Valencia observed:

"The real value of a portfolio does not lie in its physical appearance, location, or organization; rather it is in the mindset that it instills in students and teachers. Portfolios represent a philosophy that demands that we view assessment as an integral part of our instruction, providing a process for teachers and students to use to guide learning" (1990, 340).

Several general values and applications of portfolios follow.

• Portfolios are a more authentic assessment representing students' actual learning experiences and providing evidence of performance beyond the acquisition of factual knowledge.

• Portfolios accent both process and products through students' self-reflections and by providing teachers opportunities to discuss with students what they are trying to do. When teachers observe something which is unclear or seems off-task, they are encouraged to ask the student about it. *"Tell me what you're thinking about. Help me understand your thinking"* (Kingore, 1990).

• Portfolios provide opportunities for improved student self-image as accomplishments rather than deficiencies are accented (Stenmark, 1991).

• Portfolios increase students' responsibility for their own learning as they take a more active role in selecting and reflecting on their work.

• Portfolios increase students' intrinsic motivation. Encouraging students to select their best work instills within many students the desire to perform at their highest capabilities.

• Portfolios more readily incorporate examples of a student's higher-level thinking and problem solving.

• Portfolios integrate instruction and assessment. Maeroff (1991) poses the analogy that assessment drives instruction and instruction drives assessment, much as the front and rear axles impel one another in a four-wheel drive vehicle.

• Portfolios are a valuable instructional tool as teachers use portfolios to monitor class progress, provide feedback to students and parents and share information with other teachers. By analyzing portfolio contents over time, patterns of students' abilities and needs are revealed.

• Portfolios encourage a collaborative effort between teachers and students, rather than delegating assessment as the isolated responsibility of the teacher (Tierney, Carter, & Desai, 1991).

• Products may be systematically collected by all students and used to provide broad-based comparisons and self-growth indications throughout the year.

• Portfolios may be used as a means of encouraging and verifying excellence in products produced in classroom work.

• Portfolios help to increase educators' awareness of multiple kinds of student abilities by revealing a wider range of skills and understandings.

• Portfolios help to increase awareness of the abilities of special populations by providing clues to the higher abilities of some minority students which might not have shown up yet on standardized tests.

• Portfolios encourage teachers to advocate for students.

• Portfolios allow students to become their own advocates through assessing and selecting their best work and reflecting about their development and accomplishments.

• Portfolios increase inclusion instead of exclusion in gifted identification and programs by providing opportunities for every student to demonstrate gifted potential.

• Portfolios can be used as one assessment of the effectiveness of a school's or district's program, as in the Vermont State Assessment Program (Vermont, 1990).

Conferencing with Portfolios

Portfolios have important conferencing functions for students. Grant Wiggins (1989) reminds us that the root of "assessment" means to "sit with" a learner and ensure that the student's responses really mean what they seem. By talking with individual students, teachers can seek explanation, elaboration or substantiation about both the products and the process students do in learning situations. There are four key objectives in a portfolio conference between student and teacher.

1. To help the teacher learn as much as possible about student's ability, progress, needs, interests and habits.

2. To help the student reflect about his/her ability, progress, needs, interests and habits so he/she can assume responsibility for successes and needed improvements.

3. To build on the student's successes by providing encouragement and positive feedback.

4. To guide student's development of specific process goals, product goals, and timelines to complete those goals.

Talking with students about their portfolios should be an on-going process throughout the school year. Spontaneous sharing occurs as teachers move about the classroom and interact with students as they work. Periodically, however, most teachers choose to meet briefly with each student to review the portfolio, discuss his/her progress, and identify areas where additional help or encouragement may be needed. These portfolio conferences require about ten minutes per student and allow the teacher and student to collaboratively review the portfolio every several weeks.

To schedule this conferencing process, some teachers use a monthly calendar and write in one student's name on each day of the week with the goal of then being able to review portfolios with one student each day. This management device enables teachers to consistently rotate among all of the students without overextending the time available in already busy classrooms. Conferencing begins after a month or two of portfolio implementation when students have selected sufficient products to discuss. In a self-contained classroom where teachers start conferencing after the first month and schedule one student a day, students will have four or five individual conferences by the end of the year.

In departmentalized situations where teachers have multiple sections of students, teachers reported success in scheduling one ten-minute conference a class period 2 or 3 times a week, when other students were completing independent work. This resulted in most students having two individual conferences a year. A second scheduling alternative is to hold 15-minute small group conferences once a week in each class. These group conferences involve the teacher with 3-5 students and typically have a topic agenda such as discussing descriptive writing or reviewing products from their work with magnets.

In this manner, portfolios are one way to help students monitor their own development. The child who is doing well has an opportunity for private moments of recognition and encouragement which in essence say, "I'm proud of you. Keep up the good work." The child who is unsure of his/her progress can, with the teacher's guidance, compare earlier works with current products to validate that growth is occurring. Children may be more motivated to keep trying when they are thus reassured they are making some progress.

Portfolio conferences also allow an able or gifted learner who is underachieving to have an opportunity to analyze his/her portfolio to determine if it truly represents best work. Gifted students are encouraged not to compare how they are doing in relation to others but rather how they are doing in relation to their potential. Some able learners become more motivated toward excellence when encouraged to select and evaluate their best works for their own portfolios.

By actively and collaboratively involving teachers and students in the collection of work and the evaluation of achievement and growth, portfolios offer opportunities to increase mutual understanding between teacher and student. As teachers use portfolios, they become more aware of and more sensitive to individual student's needs and strengths and, as Tierney (1991) noted, are better able to provide personalized instructional support for students. Portfolio conferences provide valued opportunities to have quality one-to-one interactions, to share a hug and to understand more of the whole child.

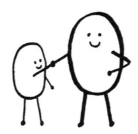

Student Preparation for a Conference

In the spirit of student ownership and responsibility, students prepare their own portfolios for a conference. The following steps are the key parts of students' preparation.

1. Students review their portfolio to verify that all selected products are in the portfolio and that the products are appropriately organized, for example, in correct chronological order.

2. They check that each product has a date on it, a reflective caption and their name.

3. Students then select one product, completed since the last conference, which they especially want to discuss with the teacher. This product will be the first thing discussed during the conference. Students typically turn this product so it extends out from the rest of the portfolio and, thus, is easy to find during the conference.

4. Some students, especially older ones, should also be encouraged to plan one or more questions or concerns they have about their work.

5. Students bring their portfolio to the conference. In some classrooms, they also bring a book they are currently reading.

Teacher Preparation for a Conference

The teacher's preparation for a conference focuses upon ensuring that the process will operate smoothly and that maximum information sharing will occur.

1. The teacher ensures that all students understand the conference procedure. It is especially important that students understand they are not to interrupt during a conference so the teacher's individual attention is focused on the student who is sharing.

2. The teacher schedules the conferences and sets up an area for the conference away from, but in clear view of, the other students.

3. The teacher also provides independent work and sufficient resources for the rest of the class to complete during the conference time.

4. Finally, the teacher brings to the conference any notes written during previous conferences with that student.

In addition, some teachers prepare a checklist to use during conferences to track the student's application of strategies or development of skills and attitudes. The checklist is meant to be diagnostic and includes items which clearly specify the behaviors or traits related to growth within a subject area. The checklist should serve to consolidate characteristics common to most students' development. However, the features on the checklist need to be thoughtfully chosen to avoid creating a narrow list of isolated skills. Many teachers reported that a checklist is best used collaboratively with the student so he/she is aware of which skills need mastery and why particular skills, strategies and attitudes are important. Used positively, a checklist is a concrete way to help students become aware of what they already know and what they need to learn next.

Guidelines for a Conference

The following guidelines for teachers serve to ensure that a student-teacher portfolio conference is as satisfying and productive a time as possible. The student is viewed as the expert regarding his/her work and the teacher is the informed listener and questioner who is interested in learning all about the products and the process of the child's development.

1. *Think of the conference as a time for sharing and conversing rather than interrogation. Emphasize just one or two teaching points during the conference. Contemplate and celebrate rather than nit-pick or lecture.*

2. *Let the student lead and dominate the conversation as much as possible. Try to listen more than you talk. Elicit the student's own perceptions of growth and needs.*

3. *Organize the conference so it is open-ended and student-centered yet has enough structure to result in the greatest amount of information -sharing in a brief amount of time.*

4. *Plan a series of leading and probing questions. The leading questions focus the student's discussion. The probing questions elicit more specific information and help the teacher learn more from the student. Examples of these questions are listed on page 41.*

5. *Recognize effort as well as achievement. Be sensitive to the effort a student may have expended to complete a product.*

6. *Incorporate as much encouragement and positive feedback as is appropriate. Accept the strengths of the portfolio. Build on what the student has accomplished. Current success frequently motivates future effort.*

7. *Collaborate with the student in goal setting. Help the student plan specific information and realistic goals to accomplish before the next conference. These goals should be different for each student and develop naturally out of the needs and interests of each. Some goals will be skill directed, e.g. "I want to master the rest of my subtraction facts so I can be faster in math." Some goals focus on expanding talents, e.g. "I'm going to work on my persuasive writing and write some editorials about the homeless." Some goals reflect personal needs, e.g. "I need to read more. I want to finish the Narnia series by C.S. Lewis."*

8. *End the conference with a moment or two for both the student and the teacher to write notes about the conference and future goals. These notes may be written on plain paper or on a simple form such as the one on the next page. A brief record of each conference is needed to prompt thinking for the next conference and to provide continuity. Writing notes at the end instead of during the conference allows the teacher to maintain more eye contact with the student as he or she shares information.*

The student's notes are typically stored in the front of the student's portfolio. However, some teachers found it useful to have students write their conference notes on colored paper and file it after the last product discussed during the conference. The colored paper, thus, clearly signaled which work has been produced since the last conference.

Most teachers keep their notes in a separate file. As a simple management technique, a teacher has a separate page for conference notes for each student and adds to that page during each conference. When a conference is completed, the teacher files that student's page in the back of the teacher's file so the student's sheets remain in the same sequence as the conference rotation schedule. The form for Conference Notes is on the next page. It may be used by the teacher, student or both.

Conference Notes ✍

Student Name _____

Conference 1   Date:

Talked about:

What has been learned:

Next goal:

Conference 2   Date:

Talked about:

What has been learned:

Next goal:

Conference 3   Date:

Talked about:

What has been learned:

Next goal:

Conference 4   Date:

Talked about

What has been learned:

Next goal:

Conference Questions

The following are examples of the types of leading questions and probing questions a teacher might plan as the guiding structure for a conference with a student. A teacher might develop additional questions to expand these and then choose a few to use at any one conference setting.

1. What have you chosen to share with me first?

    Why did you choose this product?

    What do you want to tell me about it?

    How did you think of that idea?

2. Do you have any questions or concerns you've planned to discuss today?

    What is the problem as you see it?

    How can I help?

3. What in your portfolio shows something important you've learned in _____?
    (curriculum area)

    Why do you think this product/skill is important?

    What do you feel is a strength of this work?

    What did you do to learn it?

    How did others help you?

4. Tell me about something on your reading review.

    Tell me some more about why it is important to you.

    Have you encouraged others to read it too?

    Have you read anything else like it?

    What do you plan to read next?

5. What is something you can do now that you could not do well before?

    What did you do to learn it?

    How are you using this ability?

6. What was the goal you set during our last conference?

    How have you progressed on that goal?

    How/when did you achieve it?

    What changes have you noticed in your work?

    What additional help or resources do you need?

7. Think about what goal you want to achieve next or what you want to learn next.

    Why do you think that goal is important?

    How might you start?

    How can I help?

Conferencing with Peers

In addition to student-teacher collaboration, students review their portfolio at many other times to think about it or to share it with a classmate. In some classrooms, teachers found it beneficial to organize peer conferences. All of the students in the class would simultaneously meet in groups of four or five to talk about their portfolios. Each student planned one product to share with the group, inviting conversation about the process and personal interest in that product. Students benefitted from seeing each others work and having a peer audience for their products. They also gained ideas for future work. The accent during peer conferences was to share rather than to criticize; the intent was to engender in students a respect for each others work and progress. Peer conferences generally took about fifteen minutes and occurred several times during the year as appropriate to the interest and needs of the group.

Peer conferences may also be used as a time for students to provide simple written feedback to one another. Each student should think about the product being shared in terms of its strengths and one suggestion. Students then fold a small paper in half and write their responses to each other.

Strength	*Suggestion*

Parent-teacher Conferences

Portfolios also have important conferencing functions for parents by providing parents with directly observable products and understandable evidence concerning their child's performance. Grant Wiggins (1990) applauded this advantage of portfolios by noting that the quality of student work, as displayed in that student's portfolio, is more discernible to laypersons than if we had to rely on translations of talk about stanines and renorming. The teachers in this project found nothing more effective in parent communication and in increasing parents' understanding of child development than sharing and discussing a child's portfolio with a parent. The concrete examples of work in the portfolio enabled a parent to comprehend the progress, achievements and needs of the child. Parents left a conference thinking "You really know my child," instead of "You like (or do not like) my child."

Portfolio conferences invite a more cooperative or collaborative environment for parents and teachers. Most teachers arranged the conference area so the adults sat side-by-side rather than on opposite sides of a desk. This situation allowed more comfortable sharing of examples and encouraged conversations about the child.

Continuing the attitude of student ownership, most teachers had each student select one product they especially wanted the teacher to share with the parent. Students could list any features of the product they wanted a parent to notice in addition to the reflective caption already attached to the product. This product typically became the first thing discussed during the conference and it allowed the teacher a most comfortable opening for the parent conference: *Let's begin by looking at one example of work which your child wanted me to show you first."*

A second conferencing technique proved very effective in helping a parent focus on how the child has progressed in relation to earlier levels of achievement. Teachers named the technique "Triples" because it involved selecting three representative products from a child's portfolios. The teacher chose one product from the beginning, middle and end of that part of the school year being reviewed in the conference. The teacher then briefly discussed each product in the order it was completed by the child. The three products reassured parents that growth was happening and helped them concentrate on accomplishments over time rather than just current deficiencies. The remainder of the conference than proceeded in an exchange of information between parent and teacher as appropriate to the individual student.

Child-Parent Portfolio Sharing

Both parents and children benefit from opportunities for children to directly share their portfolio with their parents or other significant family member. Children leading a sharing time with a parent accents the children's feelings of ownership of their portfolio and increases their responsibility for the quality of the work. The child, in essence, is saying: "This is mine. It is important to me and I want to share it with you." Parents benefit from being active listeners and viewing the work of school through the child's eyes.

Students prepare for the portfolio sharing by reviewing their own portfolios and planning what they want to say and share.

1. They check that the products are complete, dated, captioned and clearly organized.

2. They select the first product they want to show their parent and think about what they want to say about it. That product can have a note attached so it extends from the product and is easily found during the sharing.

3. Students then select three or four more products they want to share. Each product can have attached a note and a number indicating the order in which the products will be shared.

4. Students also reflect on their portfolio as completed thus far and think about what they like and don't like so they can share their thinking with the parent.

5. As a final preparation and confidence builder students might work in pairs and role-play the portfolio sharing process.

Child-parent portfolio sharing can occur at home or at school. Home sharing is initiated by the child taking the portfolio home at designated times to review with a parent or other interested family members. A letter and a response sheet for parents, such as the examples on pages 46 and 47, need to be included to increase parents' understanding of their role in this process. In this instance, the portfolio typically is taken home one afternoon and returned the next morning. It is especially important to send home a note alerting parents in advance of the upcoming event. A sample note may be found on the top half of page 48.

Child-parent portfolio sharing at school is best organized as a time when parents or other significant family members are invited to the classroom to meet with their children. This opportunity could be incorporated as a part of the school's open house activities or could be a separate occasion. Bottom half of page 48 includes a sample note extending an invitation to come to school to view the portfolio.

Some classrooms experienced the highest level of participation when the sharing time was arranged as a portfolio party during the noon hour. This time enabled working parents or family members to stop by the classroom for a part of their lunch hour to meet their child. Children generally needed 15 to 20 minutes to share their portfolios. It is wise to arrange for a few additional interested adults to attend the portfolio party. Then, if a family member is unavailable, each child might still have an adult with whom to share the portfolio.

This sharing time should conclude with the adult listener writing a note to the child or completing a response form for the child, such as the form on page 47. These responses and individual recognition were so important to children that most of the children filed the adult response in their portfolio to re-read and savor.

Date_____

Dear Parent(s),

Your child is eager to share this portfolio with you. As you review the portfolio together, please remember that your child has worked very hard to complete this portfolio. It contains what your child has chosen as some of his or her best work and shows how much has been learned and accomplished since the beginning of this school year.

Consider the following suggestions to ensure a positive experience for your child.

1. Let your child lead the portfolio sharing.
   Ask: *"What do you want to show me first?"*

2. Other questions you might ask your child are:
   a. *What kinds of work do you most like to do?*
   b. *How do you get some of your ideas?*
   c. *Which product in your portfolio is your favorite? Why?*
   d. *What are your next goals?*

3. Find as many positive points to respond to as possible. Encouragement will help your child know you are proud of what he or she has learned. Your positive feedback will help your child feel eager to share with you again at a later time.

4. Please complete a Portfolio Response sheet for your child. It is a special opportunity to write a note of recognition to your child.

If you have questions or concerns about anything you see or hear, please write or call me so we can discuss them together.

Thank you for participating in your child's education.

Sincerely,

_____

PORTFOLIO RESPONSE

Date: _____

I want to thank _____ (Name of child)
for sharing a portfolio with me.

One of the products I especially enjoyed was

_____

because _____

_____ .

What I liked about the whole portfolio was

_____

_____ .

I think _____ (Name of child) **should continue to**

_____

_____ .

Other questions or comments:

_____

_____

_____ .

Thank You,

_____
Signature

Sample Note: Portfolio Review at Home

Date _____

Dear Parent(s),
     Your child will bring home his/her portfolio to share with you on _____ (date). Please plan now to set aside 15 minutes to review the portfolio together so it may be returned to school the next day. This is a special opportunity for you to model to your child that school and learning are very important to you.

     To encourage organization and responsibility, help your child handle the products carefully and return the portfolio the next school day.

               Sincerely,

               _____

✂ - ✂ - ✂ - ✂ - ✂ - ✂ - ✂ - ✂ - ✂ - ✂ - ✂ - ✂ - ✂ - ✂ - ✂ - ✂

Sample Note: Invitation to Portfolio Party

Date _____

Dear Parent(s),

     You are invited to a portfolio party. Please come to our class on _____.
Your child has prepared a portfolio of his/her most important work and would like to spend 10-15 minutes showing you how much is being learned.

               Sincerely,

               _____

Evaluation of Portfolios for All Students

Each school district needs to develop its own procedures and forms for the summative evaluation of students' collected works and spontaneous products. Unless evaluation criteria and forms are carefully thought out and clearly developed, concerns about unreliability, inconsistency or inequity will emerge. Valencia admonishes that "while the flexibility of the portfolio is one of its greatest assets, it may also be one of its greatest problems" when it comes to evaluation (1990, 339).

The summative evaluation of portfolios focuses on more than just the concluding level of achievement of each student. There are four dimensions that are important to assess in the final review of each portfolio. They are:

1. The effort and productivity of the student, e.g., the quantity and quality of the student's work;

2. The student's attitudes toward learning and interests in specific topics and content areas;

3. The student's implementation of learning strategies appropriate to certain content area;

4. The student's application of designated content area skills.

Criteria may be developed in each content area to assess these dimensions in a specific and quantifiable manner.

While some evaluation examples are helpful, specific descriptions of assessment standards will vary as portfolios reflect the instructional goals of each situation (Stenmark, 1991). A selected team of educators meeting together and determining specific criteria ensures that the portfolio assessment is consistent with district goals and priorities and appropriate to the student population.

In portfolio assessment, evaluation forms need to be inclusive but succinct - inclusive of major criteria but in a succinct form to facilitate implementation. As much as possible, the criteria also need to be applicable to multiple grade levels, thus allowing the assessment criteria to remain constant across the grades while the developmental level of the children and the level of sophistication of the products change. Sample evaluation forms for math (page 50), reading (page 51), and writing (page 52) are included, not as actual forms to use but rather as prompts for developing your own holistic evaluations of product samples. The forms present a variation of formats for your consideration.

Mathematics Portfolio Criteria: Summative Evaluation Form

Student _____

School _____

At a developmentally appropriate level for the grade involved,
the portfolio products reviewed showed evidence to the extent indicated.

Key: **R** - Rarely **S** - Somewhat
  C - Consistently **N/A** - Not applicable

Grade Levels: First Semester/Second Semester

	K1	K2	11	12	21	22	31	32	41	42	51	52	61	62
Communication														
1. Uses mathematical vocabulary and notation correctly														
2. Expresses the thinking and processing involved in a problem														
3. Develops charts and graphs to organize mathematical data														
Concepts														
4. Understands the task or problem														
5. Exhibits growth in concept development														
6. Applies mathematical concepts appropriately														
7. Connects and applies mathematics to real world situations														
Problem Solving														
8. Chooses appropriate strategy to approach solving problems														
9. Recognizes assumptions and missing or extraneous data														
10. Successfully carries out the procedure														
11. Draws logical conclusions and looks back to verify														
Affective Domain														
12. Enjoys math and mathematical challenges														
13. Willingly invents, discovers, explores and integrates mathematical concepts														
14. Exhibits flexibility and risk taking in exploring mathematical alternatives														
15. Willing to persevere														
Other														
16.														
17.														
18.														

Reading Portfolio Criteria: Summative Evaluation Form

Student _____ Grade _____ Teacher _____ Date_____

At a developmentally appropriate level for the grade indicated, the portfolio products showed evidence to the extent circled under each criteria.

1. Enjoys listening and analytically responding to literature.
   Rarely   Sometimes   Frequently   Extensively

2. Reads and comprehends environmental print and predictable materials.
   Rarely   Sometimes   Frequently   Extensively

3. Exhibits fluency and expression when reading aloud.
   Rarely   Sometimes   Frequently   Extensively

4. Reads for information and enjoyment.
   Rarely   Sometimes   Frequently   Extensively

5. Self-selects a wide variety of reading materials.
   Rarely   Sometimes   Frequently   Extensively

6. Self-monitors; corrects own reading based on meaning.
   Rarely   Sometimes   Frequently   Extensively

7. Exhibits progress in reading level and ability from earlier to current evaluation.
   Rarely   Sometimes   Frequently   Extensively

8. Exhibits increasing confidence in own reading ability.
   Rarely   Sometimes   Frequently   Extensively

9. Other: _____
   Rarely   Sometimes   Frequently   Extensively

10. Check the word identification strategies successfully incorporated when reading:

   ____ applies personal schema

   ____ uses context clues

   ____ has sight word fluency

   ____ uses phonics
        skills demonstrated:

   ____ uses structural analysis
        skills demonstrated:

Writing Portfolio Criteria: Summative Evaluation Form

Student _____ Grade ____ Teacher _____ Date_____

Review the written products in a portfolio. Considering the developmentally appropriate level for the grade involved, place a check in the most applicable column to designate the degree of quality for the products. Total the number of checks in each column times the points listed. Then total all the columns.

	Low		Moderate		High	
Degree of Quality	1	2	3	4	5	6
Originality of Thought Imagination; creative fluency; emotional quality; focus; style.						
Organization Suitable to purpose; exhibits unity; clearly developed; transitions; communicates clearly.						
Mechanics Appropriate usage, structure, grammar, punctuation, spelling.						
Additional Elements Analogy; literary devices; dialogue; sense of personal expression.						
Growth Progress from earlier works; evidence of revision & development.						
Productivity: Enjoys and initiates own writing; range of writing challenges.						
Other:						
Column Total						

Total Score: _____

Know the Child and Understand the Process Before Evaluating a Product

It is important that educators know the child and understand the process a child goes through to produce a specific product. Indeed, the most valid and defensible evaluation of the merits of a product follows observation of the student as the product is being developed. Input from the child adds information and clarifies any questions.

As we evaluate portfolios, we strive to avoid leaping to conclusions and overgeneralizing about a product. Instead, we continually seek specific information about the child and the process. To evaluate a product as typical of a child's potential, we must analyze the product in the context of the whole child. For example, one member of an evaluation team was concerned about the grammatical errors in a fifth grader's work until informed that the student was from Laos and had only been speaking English for eighteen months.

Many times, input from the child is necessary to accurately interpret a product. On one occasion, a third grade child wrote a poem during some free time at school and showed it to the substitute teacher saying she wanted the teacher to see her best writing. The substitute was very excited about the quality of the poem and left it for the regular teacher. When the regular teacher asked the child about creating more poems, the child clarified that she didn't "make up" the poem; she had just "written" it. The child was not trying to deceive anyone. She innocently was trying to demonstrate one skill (handwriting) which others misinterpreted as another skill (creative writing).

As teachers try to know children more thoroughly and understand the learning process more specifically, they ongoingly observe children at work and frequently ask questions when they observe something which is unclear or seems off-task. Teachers request more information from children through questions and sentences such as the following:

Tell me about your picture.

Tell me about your work.

What are you thinking?

Tell me some more to help me understand your thinking.

Explain what you mean.

Tell me how you did that.

Tell me how you made that.

What did you do to figure that out?

What Happens to Portfolios at Year's End?

In some portfolio projects the entire portfolio is passed on to next year's teacher. That option has the advantage of providing a more complete record of a student's growth and achievements but the disadvantage of storage problems as several years' products are gathered. In addition, many teachers reported that they didn't need such a large volume of products passed to them from previous teachers. Rather, they most benefited from a smaller selection of products which reflected the student's attitudes, levels of thinking, and academic growth over a period of time.

In reality, then, the portfolio can serve a different purpose during the year from its purpose at the end (Paulson, Paulson & Meyer, 1991). Throughout the year, a range of works is collected because the products are important to the student, reflective of the student's activities and standards, and instructionally significant. At the end of the year, however, these works can be refined to a small body representative of the year's experiences and achievements. Students also benefit from a year-end review of their portfolio to determine which material they most want shared with others. Thus, we found it most productive for students and teachers to collaboratively review the portfolio to retain a few of the products for a school career portfolio and then send the remaining products home for family enjoyment.

School Career Portfolios

Teachers and students should collaboratively review portfolios at the end of the school year and select 4 to 8 products to be placed in the student's School Career Portfolio. This process is consistent with the year-end results of several portfolio projects (Chapman, 1990; Paulson, Paulson & Meyer, 1991; Vermont Department of Education, 1990). The specific number of selected products depends on the needs of the student, but these works should represent the following:

1. *At least one product from every two-three months of the school year to reflect growth through the year.*

2. *First draft(s) as well as revised and corrected copy to show the process of the student's thinking.*

3. *Products from integrated, complex and challenging tasks designed to elicit higher-level thinking and allow grade level and even above grade-level work.*

4. *Non-written products such as graphics, audio or video tapes, computer products and photographs accompanied with written explanations of three-dimensional work.*

5. *At least one product judged by the student to be his/her highest accomplishment or best piece of work. This product should be accompanied with the student's reflection - written or dictated - of why or how this is the best work and the process by which the work was completed.*

These categories are not exclusive. Frequently, one product serves to represent more than one category. The School Career Portfolio thus becomes a showcase portfolio that is added to at the end of each year and passed from one year's teacher to the next to provide an overview of the student's level of achievement and growth. These School Career Portfolios are typically stored with each student's cumulative file.

As an exciting product for the future, we envision this School Career Portfolio being bound and presented to the student at high school graduation as a record - in chronological order - of that student's productivity and accomplishments throughout his/her school career. All students do not remain in the same district for all of their school years, of course, but whatever products have been collected could be shared in this manner. The portfolio would be forwarded for any student who transfers to another school to help that new school more quickly become aware of the student's abilities and instructional needs.

Toward the end of the senior year in high school, the students culminate the School Career Portfolio process. Students develop a title page, dedication page and table of contents for their portfolios. They then write a final reflection of their school experiences as the concluding entry to their portfolio before their School Career Portfolio is bound. A student who has remained in one district the entire 13 years of school would thus have 50 or more products in the bound School Career Portfolio.

Products Not Selected for the School Career Portfolios

The bulk of the products in each student's portfolio has been used throughout the current school year to guide assessment, focus communication, motivate excellence and increase self esteem and positive attitudes toward learning. Thus, these products have already served a major function of portfolios. The products not selected for the School Career Portfolio should be sent home with the student at the end of the year.

Consider having students organize these products into a book to give to their parents. The goal of the books is to provide an organized record of the student's work throughout the year, and to include as many specific parts of books as can appropriately be incorporated as students organize their products into a more complete or "published" form. As appropriate to the age and ability of each child, the following procedures can be elaborated or simplified to create this special book. Students may:

1. Cut their portfolio file folder on the fold line to create the front and back cover for the book.

2. Write a title page complete with an inventive "publishing company" and copyright year for their book. Title examples include: Memories of Mr. Wilson's Fifth Grade and My Treasury from Kindergarten.

3. Develop a table of contents, by months of the year, which lists each product in chronological order.

4. Write an "about the author" paragraph or page and try to include a photograph of the author.

5. "Bind" their book by a) using plastic bindings, b) 3-hole punching and placing in a notebook, or c) hole punching and using one or more metal rings or yarn to hold the pages together.

As an additional learning activity, older students can develop an index for their books. Creating an index encourages analysis of main ideas as an index requires students to think about the key concepts of each product.

Parents' reactions to these finished books have been very enthusiastic and positive. Parents made comments such as:

'Now I can throw away a whole drawer full of papers. The whole year is in this one book!'

'You must really care about my child to have kept and organized this work for us.'

'We can keep this forever. It is a most treasured book on our bookshelf.'

Parents reported that children were very proud of these books. Several parents mentioned that their child looked through the book again and again. Younger children often wanted to show their book to friends and significant adults in addition to a parent. Thus, this final use of the portfolio products has the potential to extend good feelings among teachers, parents, and children and perhaps even help children retain more of what they have learned as they review their work again and again.

Question from Teachers about the Portfolio Process

1. What are the best kinds of products to include in the portfolios?

That answer will vary depending on the needs, interests and abilities of your students. The best products are those which reflect the whole child and that child's growth and development. Some general suggestions of products to include are listed pages 16 and 17.

2. Won't children make mistakes in filing their products in their portfolios?

Children often surprise us by how much they rise to our level of expectations. Generally, teachers report that even young children do well in filing their own products because they know their portfolio well and it is important to them. If occasionally a product is misfiled, it will be found as children and/or teachers review the portfolios from time to time.

3. Can products in the portfolio be redone if children want to do them over to improve the quality?

Products from the beginning of the year should not be redone or replaced later in the year because that would limit our ability to view the student's growth demonstrated over time. However, when a child asks, you might choose to allow him/her to redo a product within a day or so of the original product collection if the child is displeased with the quality of the product and wants to do it again to make it better. We do want children to feel pride in their portfolio. One ongoing goal is that the portfolio represents students' best work and motivates them to excel.

4. What if a child wants to put multiple examples of the same product in the portfolio?

Children often practice the same thing repeatedly as they perfect skills. For example, many children draw the same or nearly the same houses, planes, trucks or people over and over. Talk with that child about choosing items that are different from the other products in the portfolio. The questions for student selection discussed on page 21 may also help.

5. How can we find time to do all of this?

Time is a precious commodity in our classes. Beginning the portfolio process may require extra time until we gain skills in portfolio organization and management. With more experience implementing portfolios, however, teachers found that the key was using time *differently* rather than using more time. For example, time is saved by encouraging students to take the responsibility for most of the filing and management of the portfolio itself. Furthermore instructional time is gained as teachers find new alternatives to former practices, such as 1) using some cooperative group work instead of relying only on individual paperwork; 2) applying more techniques which accent student thinking instead of lengthy written products; 3) including more holistic learning tasks instead of the myriad of worksheets accenting isolated skill practice; and 4) incorporating techniques which increase student thinking without extensive teacher preparation of materials.

Portfolios do necessitate time and energy. But, teachers generally report that the benefits of increased student motivation, concrete evidence of student progress and more specific data to share during parent, student and teacher conferences greatly outweigh the efforts expended.

6. Isn't this just like work folders? I've always done that for my kids.

As teachers discuss this point, several differences are frequently expressed.

1. In the past, product collection and evaluation were somewhat random. Portfolios represent a more focused, consistent and systematic collection of products throughout the entire year.

2. Students are encouraged to have a much more active role in selecting portfolio items and using the products in self-analysis.

3. Portfolios typically incorporate more than one curriculum area; work folders frequently involve products from one subject, such as writing.

4. A larger body of educators now acknowledge the importance and value of alternative forms of assessment. Hence, the evaluation of portfolios is typically completed with standards established by a collaboration of educators throughout the school or district instead of each teacher determining individual evaluation criteria. Thus, portfolios may be more relevant for assessment.

5. Portfolios provide a means for districts to use this valuable product information in screening students for gifted programs.

7. I'm not sure I will be able to collect portfolio products. My children always want to take their things home.

It is important that we share with children at the beginning of the school year that the portfolio is going to show their best work, their growth throughout the year and become a special book to give their family at the end of the year. Once the portfolio is introduced, many children become so proud of their work they *want* to put it in their portfolios. As the momentum developed, teachers found that children would specifically ask if certain products could go in their portfolio. On the other hand, a teacher may always choose to make a legible photocopy of a product for the child who really wants to take a particular product home.

8. Who decides what goes in the portfolio?

Students make most of the selections to increase their pride and ownership in the portfolio. As students make their choices they demonstrate self-evaluation and decision-making skills. These are certainly important life skills. Teachers, however, may choose some products to ensure that a consistent overview of curriculum content and student growth can be demonstrated. (The discussion on pages 20-23 elaborates these points.)

9. The parents in the area where I teach aren't likely to send anything to school.

The portfolio process can still be successful and useful without any parent cooperation. Home involvement is an asset but not a necessity. What is most important is that the school environment encourage the excellence of every child and provide multiple opportunities to validate the achievements of every child.

Notes & Comments

Portfolios:
Identifying
the
Gifted

Portfolios: Identifying Gifted Students

Portfolios can also function as one criterion in the identification of gifted children. Although not frequently applied in this capacity, portfolios offer unique opportunities in the identification of gifted potentials. Because all students develop portfolios, the portfolio process allows every student to be screened for the level of products he/she produces. Minority, handicapped and economically disadvantaged students are not overlooked because *every* student assembles a portfolio for assessment. Inasmuch as portfolios include a wide range of materials and contents, the portfolio process can also screen for multiple talents and multiple types of giftedness.

Portfolio products which incorporate complex, in-depth content provide every student opportunities to demonstrate abilities to think, to solve problems, to create and to excel in his/her selected works. Thus, through portfolios, educators have an opportunity to increase their awareness of the gifted potential of students from special populations and of multiple kinds of students' abilities. In this manner, then, portfolios increase inclusion instead of exclusion in gifted identification by providing multiple opportunities for every student to demonstrate gifted potential.

Portfolios also offer classroom teachers the opportunity to be directly involved in the identification of gifted students through planning and directing activities which elicit gifted behaviors, and evaluating products resulting from those experiences. This teacher involvement further increases the likelihood that the identification process provides information that is instructionally useful instead of just a means to an end. Sylvia Rimm (1984) noted that identification should provide information which is useful for planning instruction and/or counseling gifted students. A gifted student's portfolio most certainly proves useful in both instructional planning and individual counseling.

To maximize the value of portfolios as one criterion in the process of identifying gifted students, a third category of products called planned experiences should be collected. In addition to the collected work and spontaneous products previously discussed, products from planned experiences provide relevant information and insight into the giftedness of students.

Planned Experiences

A planned experience is a special component in the portfolio process to assist in gifted identification. Planned experiences are sets of high-level, open-ended activities designed specifically to elicit and diagnose gifted behaviors since teachers vary in the degree of day-to-day stimulation and challenge they provide.

Several districts wanted some activities which all grade-level teachers complete with every student to provide equal opportunities for advanced behaviors to emerge.

Planned experiences are not needed when a district's curriculum is differentiated and designed to ensure that high-level behaviors can emerge in every classroom. However, if differentiation in all classrooms is not complete, a district can ensure that opportunities are being provided in every classroom for gifted behaviors to emerge by selecting several planned experiences to include in its curriculum.

Multiple examples of planned experiences for kindergarten through sixth grade are included in this book. These planned experiences have been field tested nationally and revised over a three-year period by hundreds of classroom teachers as part of the use of portfolios to enrich all children and identify the gifted children. Each planned experience is designed to be developmentally appropriate to a specific grade level. Each uses simple and readily available materials. Several planned experiences are based on literature for children because quality literature has so many higher-level applications and most teachers and students love good literature activities.

Each planned experience also incorporates several gifted characteristics to ensure multiple opportunities for each gifted behavior to emerge. The Organization Chart on page 115 specifies for each planned experience the intended grade level(s) and the gifted characteristics which might be elicited by that activity. In field testing, districts found that using three to six planned experiences added valued information to the rest of the portfolio data when products were being evaluated as one criterion in the identification of gifted children.

Specific directions and procedures are written for the administration and interpretation of each planned experience so that the activity and its scoring has standards which are consistently applied every time it is used. Thus, planned experiences are intended as a common denominator which guarantee several equal opportunities for every student in each grade level of a district to demonstrate gifted potential.

In addition to the planned experiences included in this book, a district can design and field test its own set of activities to elicit behaviors typical of gifted students. Developing its own planned experiences allows a district to design planned experiences which thoroughly incorporate district and curriculum goals, teacher preferences and specific population needs. Additional planned experiences may be developed by district teachers and administrators using the format and procedures on pages 88 and 89.

Gifted Characteristics Elicited by Planned Experiences

Characteristics of gifted children should serve not only to guide in the identification of gifted students but also to assist educators in organizing enriching environments for children. As Long and Clemmons observed:

"A list of characteristics of the gifted...should suggest curriculum modifications in order to meet the learning needs of the gifted. It should...be used as a guide to creating learning activities in which potentially gifted students can display the various characteristics." (1982,38).

Thus, the planned experiences in this book are designed to elicit specific behaviors characteristic of gifted children. The characteristics are those employed in the Kingore Observation Inventory (Kingore, 1990). A brief explanation of those seven categories of characteristics follows.

Advanced Language
The student unassumingly and appropriately displays an advanced vocabulary and an ability to use more complex language effectively in a variety of situations; naturally uses similes, metaphors and analogies to express relationships.

Analytical Thinking
The student demonstrates an ability to discern components of a whole; strives to determine relationships and patterns in procedures, experiences, ideas, and/or objects. The student may not be "organized", yet enjoys organizing and planning events and procedures.

Meaning Motivated
The student shows curiosity and an inner drive for thorough, independent understanding; typically asks penetrating, intellectual questions and demonstrates an extensive memory.

Perspective
The student displays an ability to understand and incorporate unexpected or unusual points of view through oral language, writing, manipulatives and/or art.

Sense of Humor
The student demonstrates understanding of higher levels of humor and application of a finely developed sense of humor, either through production of original jokes, riddles, puns, or other humorous effects or through understanding the subtle humor of others.

Sensitivity
The student is intensely sensitive to the needs of others, demonstrates a strong sense of justice and sets high standards for self and others.

Accelerated Learning
The student demonstrates mastery and an ability to learn and understand material and concepts beyond the facts and knowledge typical and expected for that age group.

The Organization Chart on page 115 plots the characteristics elicited by each planned experience. The Organization Chart is intended to assist educators in selecting planned experiences which are appropriate to desired grade levels while providing opportunities to elicit a balance of the characteristics of gifted children.

Guidelines for Selecting Planned Experiences

❑ Planned experiences are not intended to be used as a separate criterion. Rather, they are designed to be combined with the information gained from the collection and assessment of other products throughout the school year. Incorporating collected work samples, spontaneous products and planned experiences increases the value and reliability of the information used to identify gifted potential.

❑ In the majority of field testing, school district personnel chose three to six planned experiences to incorporate in the portfolio part of their gifted identification process. These planned experiences were typically administered one every week or one every two weeks. Some districts, however, varied the number and schedule to match their situations, resources, available time, and other information sources.

❑ In keeping with the spirit of considering multiple sources of information and providing several opportunities for students to demonstrate the varied facets of their potential, using less than three planned experiences is not recommended and using four to six planned experiences is preferred.

❑ Select the specific number and type of planned experiences which will most effectively supplement the rest of the information you are collecting.

❑ Choose experiences that use the skills most compatible with the instructional objectives and curriculum contents of your gifted programs.

❑ Select a combination of planned experiences which provide children opportunities to demonstrate all of the seven categories of the gifted behaviors (KOI).

❑ Choose planned experiences which might most effectively and naturally be integrated into the regular classroom schedule and curriculum.

❑ Choose planned experiences that differentiate with higher-levels of thinking without frustrating or alienating regular learners.

❑ Districts are encouraged to develop additional planned experiences which reflect the needs, interests and talents of their student population while eliciting the specific higher-level behaviors needed for success in their type of gifted program.

❑ Be aware that the Attribute Blocks and Attribute Cards activities must be administered individually. All of the other planned experiences may be administered in whole group, small groups or individually. In field testing, many districts who individually administered one or more planned experiences reported a trade-off between the increased time for individual administration versus the amount of increased information gained from the one-to-one interactions.

Procedures for Using Planned Experiences

1. After referring to the Guidelines for the Selections of Planned Experiences (page 65), select the four to six or more planned experiences to be used.

2. Schedule the administration of the planned experiences so all grade level classes administer each planned experience at approximately the same time. To insure a fair comparison among classes, a specific planned experience does not have to be scheduled at the exact same time and date in each class, but certainly should be administered within the same week.

3. To facilitate scheduling and to have time to do these planned experiences in an already full class day, connect the completion of a planned experience to those times of the day when related content is being taught. For example, the literature, rebus stories, or problem solving with shapes might be completed as independent seat-work during language arts period; children could write their rebus stories during general writing or journal writing time.

4. Stress the importance across grade levels of consistency in the administration and use of the planned experience to ensure an equal opportunity for every student to demonstrate gifted potential.

5. Share "Suggestions for Encouraging Individuality" (see page 67) with teachers to encourage individual student responses during completion of the planned experiences.

6. Share "Suggestions for Taking Dictation from Students" (see pages 68-70) with kindergarten through first or second grade teachers.

7. Provide each grade level teacher with a copy of the directions and handouts needed to complete each of the selected planned experiences. The intended grade level of each activity is indicated to the left of the copyright symbol on each handout. Planned experiences are typically administered by the teacher in each class.

8. Have children put their names and date on the back of their planned experiences to increase the objectivity of their evaluation.

9. Avoid prompting the children beyond what is stated in the planned experience directions.

10. All the planned experiences are untimed. Allow each child as much time as needed or appropriate to encourage his/her best effort.

11. Have another independent activity ready for the children when each finishes a planned experience. While approximate times needed for completion are indicated for each experience, individual children will finish at different times.

12. When everyone in the class has finished a planned experience, collect the products and paper clip the set together. No grading or interpretation of results is necessary at this time. The planned experiences are not filed in the students' portfolios. Simply store the set of planned experiences in a safe place until all the class sets are scheduled to be brought to the grade-level evaluation team for review and scoring.

13. Planned experiences are confidential and are not sent home with students before or after the completion of the activity. Otherwise, the diagnostic potential of the planned experiences might be jeopardized.

Suggestions for Encouraging Individuality

Students sometimes look around at the work of others to reassure themselves that their idea is appropriate. Some less confident children may even follow the lead of a child who others view as successful by copying that child's ideas or product. Thus we need to encourage individuality in the students' responses to activities by verbalizing to the students that everyone has different ideas and everyone's ideas are important. Of course, we need to reinforce that statement by modeling our acceptance of different ideas and answers as frequently as it is appropriate to do so. Remind students that it is often fun to try to think of something no one else has thought of. "There is a special good feeling you get when you know you figured something out for yourself or thought of your own idea."

One suggestion for modeling and rewarding individuality throughout the school year involves the use of human graphs. Spread out pictures or objects representing the subject of graphing, e.g. different kinds of fruit. Each child chooses his/her favorite or most appropriate choice and stands in front of it. You may prefer to have the children write down or draw a quick picture of their choice first so when they get up to stand by their choice they don't change their ideas just to stand by a friend. As soon as all the children are standing in a line beside their choice, count the total of each line. Compare and discuss the results and model your encouragement of different ideas. "Six people chose apple; five people chose banana only one person chose pineapple. Eric is the only person who had that idea. It is good to have your own ideas." Other topics for human graphs include colors in clothing, favorite television programs and favorite sports.

Three additional suggestions for encouraging individual responses during the planned experiences are as follows.

1. Offices.
One suggestion to increase individuality is shared by several teachers who are using planned experiences. Some teachers report that they encourage individual thinking by creating dividers to separate work spaces for students. Folders or card-stock papers are taped together to make dividers to put up between students. To accent the positive, teachers call these dividers "offices", and tell students they can set up their offices any time they want a private moment or want to pursue individual or private work. In these classrooms, students have been heard saying to another student, "I'm going to my office to work."

2. Separate Work Areas.
A second suggestion is to arrange all or some of the students' work spaces out of the view of each other. You know your students best. There may be just a student or two who needs a separate work area.

3. Group Size.
A final suggestion to encourage individual responses is to vary the size of the group when administering a planned experience. Any planned experience may be completed in whole group, small groups or individually if you prefer to or if you have the support help to do so. It is also appropriate for planned experiences to be completed individually with any student needing special assistance, e.g. a physically handicapped student.

Teacher-directed groups or teacher-directed learning centers are the best opportunities to administer planned experiences in small group settings. For example, teachers who have centers in their classroom sometimes use center time to work with a small group of students to complete a planned experience. A teacher may wish to work on a planned experience with just one small group a day, thus completing a planned experience with all of the children over a period of three to five days.

Suggestions for Taking Dictation from Students

       Teachers, especially in kindergarten and first grade, may wish to have the children tell about their ideas while someone else writes for them. This option is particularly important whenever a teacher knows that a child's thinking or insight may not be as clear or elaborate if the child does his/her own written explanation. For example, consider the response below from a limited English speaking kindergartener. The child drew a spiral on his paper. It didn't seem especially significant until the teacher asked the child, in his native language, to tell about his picture. He proceeded to explain that it was the inner ear and he correctly told her about the three parts inside the ear.

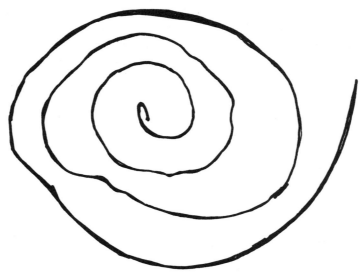

"Adentro de me' oreja — en el medio. Hay tres cosas por dentro que me ayuda oír."

"The inside of my ear--in the middle. There are three things in there that help me hear."

       Thus, recording the dictation of a child may reveal a higher level response than what appears from a more casual examination.

Dictation is initiated by using one or two verbal prompts with each child.

"Tell me about your _____."

If more explanation is desired, say:

"Tell me some more to help me understand your thinking."

> *To insure equal opportunity for all students, only a maximum of two verbal prompts may be used at any time.*

This dictation may be written by the teacher, an aide, or a volunteer selected by the teacher.

Children tend to finish activities at different times. Thus, it is seldom the case of everyone being ready to tell about his/her work at the same time. Teachers, or others taking dictation, typically set themselves in a place in the room where they can see everyone but are away from the group. As a child finishes, the child brings the work to the teacher and dictates his/her ideas. This procedure allows a better use of the teacher's time and lessens the chance of one child's dictation influencing the thinking of another child.

Additional people may be brought into the classroom to help the teacher take dictation from the students. The following suggestions for sources of additional help without additional expense were shared by teachers field testing these materials.

Parents

During the planned experiences, it is probably best not to use a parent or one of the children because of the potential for bias. Save your parent volunteers to help in another way at another time.

Senior Citizens

Some teachers use retired couples as volunteer helpers to take student dictation. In some programs, retired couples adopt a classroom for the whole school year and regularly work in that classroom to assist during projects and to provide more individual contact with the children.

Schools are sometimes located near a senior citizen center. In those cases, arrangements may be made for the center's van to bring senior citizen volunteers to the school for thirty minutes or an hour one day a week or even daily. Schools report that this alternative proves mutually beneficial and rewarding for teachers, children, and the senior citizens.

Older Students

In buildings with upper elementary or older grades, one to four older students have been used as helpers in kindergarten through second grade classrooms to take dictation. The student helpers are typically chosen because they are very able learners who can communicate well with younger children. Think how quickly the dictation process may be completed when five people instead of just one teacher write for the children!

Arrangements may be made to use those older students as student helpers during that time of the day when the rest of their class is involved in working on a skill they have already mastered. It is an asset to those students to have an alternative task such as helping younger students, instead of just repeatedly practicing something they already know well.

A few moments for training and preparing these student helpers is important. A primary teacher may arrange a fifteen -minute period, such as immediately after school, when the student helpers come to the primary classroom to meet with the teacher. During this meeting the teacher would accent:

1. The location in the room of any materials such as paper and pencils which the student helpers might need;

2. Where the student helpers are to sit to complete the dictation;

3. That the most important thing about the dictation is the *ideas* of the younger child; handwriting and spelling are less important than writing as many of the child's own words as possible.

Consider serving a beverage and cookies during this meeting. Refreshments add to the fun and comradery of the workshop.

Tape Recording

Some teachers prefer to use a tape recorder and have the children dictate their responses on tape. This can be a motivating alternative for the children because they typically enjoy using a tape recorder. Teachers should keep in mind, however, that the recorded responses generally need to be transcribed onto the children's products at some time. Thus, transcribing the tapes may ultimately take more teacher time than just taking the dictation directly from the student.

Teachers who have been tape recording student responses caution that teachers will often need to repeat certain responses a child makes during the taping. Children speak softly at times and turn their heads away from the recorder. Unless a teacher repeats statements, these ideas may be indecipherable for later analysis and transcribing.

70

Evaluation
of
Products
for
Gifted Identification

Criteria for Product Evaluation: Criteria Modes

Evaluation criteria are needed to enable educators to communicate to one another what makes one product higher-level than another or what deems one product indicative of giftedness. While multiple criteria are possible, six criteria proved the most beneficial in evaluating portfolios to assist in the identification of gifted students. The six criteria are used to label and explain the degree of gifted behaviors evidenced in a specific product or the degree of excellence educators viewed in a student product being considered.

As a mnemonic device, these criteria are referred to as criteria modes or "C Modes".

Criteria MODES

Content - exhibits in-depth understanding

Materials - clever or resourcefully used

Organization - advanced; unusual; planned

Divergence - unique or unexpected idea

Elaboration - complex; detailed; content-related

Significantly beyond age level

A more expanded explanation of each criterion is listed below.

Content - exhibits in-depth understanding
Student exhibits more depth and knowledge about the topic or subject than typical. The content may even reflect the fact that the product involves a topic seldom understood by a child of this age.

Materials - clever or resourcefully used
Student uses provided materials in a different but appropriate manner; resourceful; uses materials in an unexpected way such as making something three-dimensional when most products are two-dimensional.

Organization - advanced; unusual; planned
Student's arrangement of information on the page is different, perhaps even creative, but appropriate; for example, alphabetically organized when that was not requested. The organization might also show insightful planning in how the student arranged the information.

Divergence - unique or unexpected idea
Student's product is atypical, unlike others of this age; it may often reflect in-depth content or understanding through a very original or creative idea. It is more than just cute or weird. When looking at multiple sets of examples, this student's work stands out as unique but appropriate.

Elaboration - complex; detailed; content-related
The product has extensive detail either in words or graphics, which adds clarity or effect and is related to content. For example, a student's illustration might include lines to indicate movement, texture or patterns; a student's explanation might involve complex syntax and rich description. The elaboration, however, must add to the content rather than just be random or run-on ideas.

Significantly beyond age level
Student's product seems surprisingly advance for the age of the student; level of work is more typical of older students.

Evaluation Procedures

Evaluation Teams

Teams are formed for each grade level or, in very small districts, across several grade levels. Each team consists of several grade-level teachers plus administrators, counselors or consultant as desired who work together to score the planned experiences for those teachers' classes. It is vital that most of the individuals on a team are knowledgeable about the developmental characteristics for the age of the children whose works are being evaluated. This knowledge enables the team to more accurately determine what is typical or advanced for a designated grade level product.

Each class teacher is an active member of the team and serves as a source of additional information and insights about the students in his/her class. However, teacher bias is limited as multiple professional educators share in the process of reviewing, discussing and evaluating each product. Inter-rater reliability among evaluation team members is established through the training and particularly the scoring simulation experienced before the actual product evaluation begins.

As an alternate method, a district or school could designate a single evaluation team composed of just a few educators who evaluate all of the products from all of the classes. This single-team alternative seems simpler because a smaller number of people may be easier to schedule and train. Some districts chose this option to insure consistency and reliability.

However, field testing verified that there are many advantages when <u>all</u> teachers participate on the evaluation teams:

1. *Information provided by each classroom teacher is important and helps to clarify and interpret some products.*

2. *Teachers' awareness of the behaviors and products of gifted students is enhanced as teachers review and analyze a wider range of products than typically demonstrated in any single class.*

3. *As teachers participate on an evaluation team they view the product of a larger segment of the population and have an opportunity to better understand how diverse cultural and economic backgrounds impact the work of students. Teachers more effectively interpret work in light of their increased understanding.*

4. *Teachers increase their awareness of the wide range of abilities students exhibit and the multiple ways in which abilities may be demonstrated.*

5. *Teachers become more knowledgeable of their district's school's assessment and identification process.*

As a final verification of the value of all teachers participating on the evaluation team, see the teacher comments on page 79.

<u>Training</u>

Team members must receive training regarding the characteristics of gifted children, the criteria for product evaluation, and how to score products based upon those characteristics and criteria. This training should include a review of sample portfolios and conclude with a scoring simulation. In the simulation, a sample class set of one planned experience is displayed on overhead transparencies and reviewed simultaneously by the entire team as pairs of team members work together to practice scoring each product. Then the pairs compare scores and discuss questions and observations with the rest of the team. The simulation and discussion continue, using additional class sets as needed, until inter-rater reliability is established.

In field testing, evaluation teams consistently demonstrated 90-100% reliability using the holistic scoring procedures described in this section. The scoring simulation typically involves 20-30 minutes. The time required for the remainder of the recommended training depends on the participants' background in gifted education.

<u>Scoring</u>

Teachers take all their class portfolios and planned experiences with them to the evaluation team for review and scoring. The scoring process is discussed below and sequenced in the Evaluation Flow Chart on page 78.

How to score the planned experience(◆) will be discussed first.
Then scoring portfolio products(■) will be discussed.

◆ *Scoring Planned Experiences.*

After training, team members work in pairs to review and score class sets of planned experiences. The evaluation is mentally challenging as educators must continually analyze what student products reveal about student abilities.

Each pair needs the following materials for each planned experience they are to evaluate:

1. A copy of the evaluation guidelines and examples for each experience;

2. Class sets of completed planned experiences;

3. A scoring form for each class;

4. A copy of the directions for each planned experience. Many times it is useful to refer to the directions to determine exactly what was being required of the students.

Initially, the pair quickly looks through a class set of one planned experience to get an overview of the set. Using the appropriate evaluation guidelines and examples, the pair then goes through the same set again and scores each planned experience as either "W"* or "1" on the back of each product.

> *"W" means "wonderful child", but not demonstrating gifted criteria in that particular product. Children are wonderful and valued regardless of the degree of their abilities. In the original field testing, a score of "0" was used in this holistic evaluation. But teachers did not like to put zeros on students' papers even when the papers were not going to be seen by the students or parents. As a more positive note, we began scoring each product either "W" for wonderful child or "1" for one indicator of gifted potential.*

W = A score of " **W** " (wonderful!) is written on the back of the product if none of the criteria is indicated in the product.

1 = A score of " **1** " is written on the back of the product if one or more of the criteria are evidenced in the product.

When a score of "1" is given, the team usually tries to list by the "1" the criterion or criteria indicated in the product in order to better communicate to others why they believe the product is more indicative of giftedness (See page 72). The listed criterion or criteria do not add more value to the score but do help to clarify the thinking of the evaluators.

> *Example: a score of "1 C S" notes that the product exhibited in-depth content understanding and significantly exceeded age-level expectations.*

The majority of products typically receive a score of "W". Only a few students' products will exhibit criteria typical of the gifted as only a small percentage of the population is gifted.

Each set is then reviewed and scored by a second pair of educators. The process is complete if these four professionals agree on a score for each product. The scores are then recorded on a scoring form for that class (see page 80). All of the students in the class can be listed, or to save time, some districts just list the students who score "1". The scoring process is then repeated using the next class set.

If agreement of "W" and "1" is not reached, the product is turned sideways in the pile so it is easy to locate. When all the products in a class set have been scored, the two pairs discuss the differences and try to reach consensus. If disagreement still exists, a third pair reviews the product and discussion is encouraged. In the few cases where disagreement still exists, the product is flagged with a note attached to the product so it stands out from the rest of the set of planned experiences. Flagged products can be reevaluated later. A question mark (**?**) is recorded on the scoring form for that student's product until the product is re-evaluated.

■ *Scoring Portfolio Products*

After all of the planned experiences are scored, the evaluation team assesses the portfolios for additional indications of gifted potential in the work the students have been producing in their classes. For the purpose of gifted identification, the collected work and spontaneous products are as equal and important indicators as the planned experiences. Therefore, the portfolio is reviewed to score maximum possible points equal to the number of planned experiences that were administered. For example, if 5 planned experiences were administered, the portfolio is reviewed and products scored up to the total of 5 additional points. This procedure, in addition to equalizing the weight of planned experiences and collected work/spontaneous products, also eliminates the risk of any portfolio receiving a higher score just because it has *more* total products in it. Thus if 5 planned examples were administered, a maximum of 5 additional points is possible regardless of how many products are in the portfolio.

The holistic scoring process used with the planned experiences is now repeated using portfolio products, i.e., collected work and spontaneous products. Pairs of educators score each product "W" or "1" until either all the products are evaluated or the maximum possible points have been scored. When the maximum possible points for a portfolio is reached, the pairs of educators may conclude their evaluation of that portfolio for the purposes of gifted identification. As the evaluation of each portfolio is finished, the score is recorded on the scoring form in the collected work/spontaneous products column. That score will range from "0" (no gifted indicators) to the maximum possible points (equal to the number of planned experiences).

The team may choose to review any or all of the portfolios but especially must evaluate the portfolios of any student who scored high on the planned experiences and any student whose collected work and spontaneous products show high promise. The teachers who know children best may advocate for any child by pointing out specific product examples and elaborating with classroom anecdotes regarding a student's classroom performance. After the entire portfolio i.e., collected work, spontaneous products and all of the planned experiences, is scored for each child, the team reviews the total scores on the scoring forms and analyzes any question marks to determine if one point would make a significant difference for any child's percentile rank. If the one point is significant, the entire evaluation team discusses the product until a consensus is reached. The question mark is then crossed out and the "W" or "1" is written on the scoring form. For example, on the completed sample of the scoring form on page 81 Jacquelne's (#8) patterning product was reevaluated and scored "W"; Andreas's (#4) and Thomas' (#16) question marks were not reevaluated as they would not make a significant difference.

Finally, it is important to convert the total scores into a form which allows comparison among other gifted identification criteria. Thus, district norms may be developed (see pages 83-85) and percentiles entered by each student's total score. On the completed sample of the Scoring Form, for example, percentiles were listed using the rankings computed on the sample District Norms Form (page 85). If desired, percentiles may also be plotted on a Student Profile: Gifted Identification Form to enable comparison of the multiple criteria used by a district to complete gifted identification.

Time Requirements

Once the scoring procedures and criteria modes are clearly understood, a class set of one planned experience takes five to ten minutes to score. (Scoring time is sometimes extended because educators become so fascinated by the products that they digress and talk about the students for awhile.) To estimate the total time required to evaluate planned experiences, multiply ten minutes, times the number of classes for a grade level, times the number of planned experiences. Then double that amount because each set is reviewed by two teams. Finally, divide that amount by the number of pairs of educators on the evaluation team.

Amount of time required for planned experience evaluation =

$$\frac{\text{10 minutes x number of classes x number of planned experiences x 2}}{\text{number of pairs of educators}}$$

Example I: 5 K-1st grade classes working together

  4 planned experiences

  3 pairs of educators (5 teachers + counselor)

  $\frac{10 \text{ minutes} \times 5 \times 4 \times 2}{3}$ = 133.3 minutes (2 hrs,13 min)

Example II: 12 fifth-grade classes

  4 planned experiences

  7 pairs of educators
  (12 teachers + assistant principal + consultant)

  $\frac{10 \text{ minutes} \times 12 \times 4 \times 2}{7}$ = 137.1 minutes (2 hrs.17,min)

As examples I and II illustrate, the evaluation time requirements vary only slightly for a small number of classes or a large number of classes. As long as every class teacher is a member of the team, the proportion of the number of products to score per team member remains about the same.

The evaluation can be done in one sitting or in two or more shorter blocks of time. An additional 45-60 minutes will be needed to score the collected work and spontaneous products of all of those students who demonstrated gifted potential on the planned experiences.

Evaluation Flow Chart

1. Evaluation Team(s) review planned experiences.

Pairs of educators review a class set and score each product "1" or "W"

Second pair reviews and scores same set

Pairs Agree → Pairs Disagree

Scores recorded on scoring form → Discussion between pairs

Consensus reached → Consensus not reached

Process repeated using next class set

Third pair reviews and scores only those products lacking consensus.

Discussion

Disagreement still exists

Product is flagged with note extending from class set. A question mark (?) is temporarily recorded on the scoring form.

II. Evaluation teams(s) review the collected works and spontaneous products of
1) any student whose planned experiences indicate gifted potential, or
2) any student for whom a teacher advocates.

Pairs of educators score each product "1" or "W" until the maximum points possible* have been reached or until all of the collected works and spontaneous products for that student have been scored.

Scores are recorded on scoring form

Flagged products are reevaluated for any student for whom one point makes a significant difference. Question mark (?) on scoring form is changed to "W" or "1".

Scores from planned experiences and collected works/spontaneous products are added to determine each student's total score.

III. District norms are developed and percentiles entered by each student's total score. If desired, the percentiles may be plotted on a Student Profile form to compare multiple criteria.

For gifted identification, the maximum points possible on the collected works and spontaneous products equals the number of planned experiences that were administered, e.g., when four planned experiences are administered, up to four additional points are possible from the collected works and spontaneous products.

Teacher Comments about the Evaluation Process

The following comments were shared by teachers from several different districts after they had participated on their first evaluation team to review and score planned experiences and product portfolios.

" I learned so much about my children. One of my very quiet ones surprised me with the quality of his responses."

"On the first ones (planned experiences) you review you are so cautious. You feel as if each decision is earth shattering. Then you relax and realize you are looking at so many aspects of each child that they all work together to give you a pattern of each child's level of thinking, ability and needs. I really relaxed and enjoyed it then. It was fun to see the patterns emerge."

"This is mentally draining and exhilarating at the same time."

"There's a lot of things I want to do differently in my class now. I see so many additional ways I can encourage higher-level thinking."

"It's so interesting! I've learned to look at what children are doing in many new ways. It's going to help me work more effectively with some of my special kids."

"This has greatly influenced how I respond to children to encourage their ideas more."

"A pattern of the strengths of a child emerged after thinking about several of the products. Two or three products would not be enough to see those patterns as clearly."

"Evaluating these products showed me the difference between my high achievers and my gifted children. I saw real differences in the thinking and complexity of the gifted ones."

"One child I hadn't noticed excelled on several products. I'm going to watch her more closely and try to challenge her more in my class."

" I have a hearing impaired child. He wears hearing aids and heavy glasses. He doesn't speak up in class at all. But it was wonderful to see what he did on the planned experiences! He excelled on all of them."

(One teacher stood up at the end of the evaluation session and addressed the whole team.)
"I didn't see the need for this process and I certainly didn't want to do it! But I wanted you all to know I have changed my mind. I learned so much about my children. I realized so many things I'd never even thought about before."

SCORING FORM

School: _____

Teacher: _____

Grade: _____

Total points possible:_____

	Name of Student	Planned Experiences						Collected Work and Spontaneous Products	Total	Percentile
1.										
2.										
3.										
4.										
5.										
6.										
7.										
8.										
9.										
10.										
11.										
12.										
13.										
14.										
15.										
16.										
17.										
18.										
19.										
20.										
21.										
22.										
23.										
24.										
25.										

▫▫

SCORING FORM

School: **Franklin Elementary**

Teacher: **Ms speare**

Grade: **2**

Total points possible: **12**

	Name of Student	Attribute Classification	Patterning	Rebus Stories	Problem Solving with Shapes	What Can You Do with a Pocket?	Draw Starts	Collected Work and Spontaneous Products	Total	Percentile
		Planned Experiences								
1.	Shanna	/	/	/	/	/	w	6	11	99
2.	Jake	w	1	w	w	w	w	3	4	72
3.	Miranda	w	w	w	w	w	w	2	2	50
4.	Andrea	w	w	?	w	w	w	0	0	0-36
5.	Michael	w	w	w	w	w	w	2	2	50
6.	Zella	w	w	w	w	w	1	2	3	65
7.	Pou	w	1	w	w	w	w	0	1	37
8.	Jacqueline	1	w/	w	w	1	w	3	5	80
9.	Brandi	w	w	w	w	w	w	0	0	0-36
10.	Mustafa	1	1	w	/	1	/	5	10	98
11.	Luis	w	w	w	1	w	w	1	2	50
12.	LaTisha	1	w	w	w	w	w	1	2	50
13.	Terri	1	w	1	w	1	1	2	6	84
14.	Gregory	w	w	w	1	w	1	4	6	84
15.	Roland	w	w	1	w	w	w	2	3	65
16.	Thomas	w	1	w	w	?	w	0	1	37
17.	Sherry	w	w	w	w	w	w	1	1	37
18.	Jurel	1	1	1	w	1	w	3	7	90
19.	Micola	w	w	w	w	w	/	2	3	65
20.	Anita	w	w	w	1	w	w	3	4	72
21.	Patrick	w	w	w	w	w	w	0	0	0-36
22.	Nigel	w	w	w	w	w	w	0	0	0-36
23.	Sylvia	w	w	w	w	w	w	0	0	0-36
24.										
25.										

81

Notes & Comments

Developing District-wide Norms for Portfolio

The portfolio appropriately applies the professional judgment of teachers and other educators in evaluating student products for evidence of potential giftedness. It is recommended that each school district develop its own norms as a more valid reflection of the specific student population and subjective professional judgment of the educators in the district. Norms should be recomputed every year for the first three years and recomputed every three years, thereafter. If the student population is large (500+ per grade), norms should be established for each grade level.

The following procedure and form (pages 84,85) may prove helpful in determining local norms in percentiles. Percentiles are used because the majority of the districts in this project preferred the data in that form. However, standard scores could also be computed if a district so chose. Further information and procedures may be found in numerous statistical references such as the one listed below. A completed sample for determining district percentiles is included as one example.

Procedure

1. Using the class totals from each class' portfolio Scoring Form, determine the number of students being evaluated. Record this number (TNS) in the "Total Number of Students Evaluated" space on the District Norms Form.

Example:
20 + 21 + 22 + 23 + 20 + 24 + 22 + 23 + 20 + 21 + 24 + 21 + 19 + 20 + 22
= 322 total students evaluted (TNS).

2. For each student listed on each Scoring Form make a mark on the District Norms Form beside the number of points that student received.

(See sample District Norms Form p.81)

3. Determining total for frequencies: Total the number of marks beside each number of points on the District Norms Form. This represents the number of students receiving each number of points.

(See sample District Norms Form p.85)

4. Determining cumulative frequencies: Starting with the highest number of possible points in the District Norms Form, record the number of students receiving that number of points in the Cumulative Frequency (CF) column of the District Norms Form. Add the number of students receiving the next lower number of tallies to the CF to get a new CF. Repeat this process until the CF for each tally number has been computed.

From sample District Norms Form (p.81):
- 12+ points (1 student) CF=1
- 11 points (1 student) CF=1+1=2
- 10 points (6 students) CF=2+6+8
- 9 points (9 students) CF=8+9=17

5. Determining percentiles: Divide each CF by the total number of students evaluated (TNS). Multiply the results by 100. Subtract this percentage from 100. Record the resulting percentiles by the appropriate tally number in the Percentiles column of the District Norms Form.

From sample District Norms Form (p.81):
Percentile - (100 - 100 (CF÷TNS))
- 12+ points: [100-100 (1÷322)] = 99th percentile
- 11 points: [100-100 (2÷322)] = 99th percentile
- 10 points: [100-100 (8÷322)] = 98th percentile
- 9 points: [100-100 (17÷322)] = 95th percentile

Example by Kathy Hall and Bertie Kingore. For extended information regarding norm development, refer to Witte, Robert S. (1989). <u>Statistics </u>(3rd ed.) Fort Worth, TX: Holt, Rinehart, Wilson.

DISTRICT NORMS FORM
FOR PORTFOLIOS

District:_____   Grade Level(s):_____

Total Number Students Evaluated (TNS):____

# OF POINTS	# STUDENTS PER # OF POINTS (FREQUENCY)	TOTAL FREQUENCY	CUMULATIVE FREQUENCY (CF) (ADD FROM BOTTOM UP)	PERCENTILE $100 - \left(\dfrac{100\ CF}{TNS}\right)$	# OF POINTS
0					0
1					1
2					2
3					3
4					4
5					5
6					6
7					7
8					8
9					9
10					10
11					11
12					12

DISTRICT NORMS FORM
FOR PORTFOLIOS

District: _____   Grade Level(s): K-2

Total Number Students Evaluated (TNS): 322

# OF POINTS	# STUDENTS PER # OF POINTS (FREQUENCY)	TOTAL FREQUENCY	CUMULATIVE FREQUENCY (CF) (ADD FROM BOTTOM UP)	PERCENTILE $100 - \left(\frac{100\ CF}{TNS}\right)$	# OF POINTS
0	卌 卌 卌 卌 卌 /// 卌 卌 卌 卌 卌 卌 卌 卌 卌 卌 卌 卌 卌 卌 卌 卌 卌 卌	118	322	0-36	0
1	卌 卌 /// 卌 卌 卌 卌 卌 卌	43	204	37	1
2	卌 卌 卌 /// 卌 卌 卌 卌 卌 卌	48	161	50	2
3	卌 卌 卌 卌 ///	23	113	65	3
4	卌 卌 卌 卌 卌 /	26	90	72	4
5	卌 卌 //	12	64	80	5
6	卌 卌 卌 卌	20	52	84	6
7	卌 ////	9	32	90	7
8	卌 /	6	23	93	8
9	卌 ////	9	17	95	9
10	卌 /	6	8	98	10
11	/	1	2	99	11
12	/	1	1	99	12

85

District_____   Date_____

Student Profile:
Gifted Identification

					Above Average	Superior	Very Superior
Name_____ Grade_____				Average			
School_____							
Birthdate_____ Age___ Yr____ Mo____	%	2	16	50	84	98	99.9
Ethnic Code: (Circle) A B H N W		-2sd	-1sd	MEAN	+1sd	+2sd	+3sd
1.							
_____							
_____							
_____							
2.							
_____							
_____							
_____							
3.							
_____							
_____							
_____							
4.							
_____							
_____							
_____							
5.							
_____							
_____							
Comments/Alternate criteria							
_____							
_____							
_____							
_____							

District_____ Date _January 18, 1993_____

Completed Sample

Student Profile:
Gifted Identification

Name _Mustafa_____ Grade _2_____

School _FRANKLIN ELEMENTARY_____

Birthdate _7-9-85_ Yr _7_ Age Mo _7_

Ethnic Code: (Circle) A B (H) N W

			Average			Above Average	Superior	Very Superior
%	2	16	50	84		98		99.9
	-2sd	-1sd	MEAN	+1sd		+2sd		+3sd

1. PRODUCT PORTFOLIO
   Planned Experiences = 5
   Portfolio = 5
   total = 10
   Percentile = 98

2. Kingore Observation
   Inventory 96%

3. Comprehensive Test of Basic Skills
   Total Lang.: 85
   Total Math: 97
   Total Battery: 93

4. WISC-3
   131

5. Creativity Task
   (district NORMED INSTRUMENT)
   84

Comments/Alternate criteria
Used highest indicator
on CTBC
English Second Language

Developing Additional Planned Experiences

In addition to the planned experiences provided in this book, multiple other activities could be developed and effectively used as planned experiences. Planned experiences may be created by district teachers and administrators using the format on the next page. For maximum value, new planned experiences should be field tested in several classrooms and then carefully revised before using the activities to elicit gifted behaviors and identify potentially gifted students. This procedure, then, might parallel the process described in the Development and Field Testing Section of this book.

The following guidelines might prove helpful in developing additional planned experiences.

1. Be sure each activity is a) educationally defensible for the age group(s) involved and b) can elicit high level responses. These activities must be much more than just cute or fun activities.

2. Concentrate on choosing experiences which elicit a balance of the seven categories of gifted behaviors (Kingore, 1990).

3. Avoid activities that isolate creativity, e.g. just encourage fluency, flexibility, originality or elaboration without a content or gifted behavior connection. Children can incorporate creativity in their responses. Creativity should be subsumed -- not isolated (Kingore, 1990).

4. Try to choose activities that use skills and topics across the curriculum. Avoid too narrow a focus, e.g., overuse of drawing, overuse of writing. Consider what could be done using the content and materials from subjects such as math, social studies or science.

5. Be sure that the directions set up the experiences intended in the objective. You are less likely, for example, to get analytical thinking, in-depth understanding or complexity if you don't encourage it through the activity directions.

6. Ensure that complete bibliographic data of references is included, when applicable. Model professionalism by crediting the source of the activity or idea.

Format for Developing Planned Experiences

Grade levels _____

Title: _____

Date due: _____ Teacher: _____

Objective(s):

Students will have an opportunity to demonstrate (gifted behaviors or characteristics)

_____

by (product) _____ .

Materials

Preparing for the Activity:

Demonstrating the Activity:

Completing the Activity:

Questions from Teachers about Planned Experiences

1. I'm already swamped with things that have to be done. How can I find time to do these activities too?

Instead of "adding on" those activities to your busy day, "build them in" and incorporate them as part of your regular schedule. Plan to use the activities as part of your students' independent seat work assignments. You can give the directions and model the planned experience with the whole group and then the students can complete the activity later during their independent work time. Complete the planned experiences during appropriate subject blocks of time, e.g., patterning or attribute analysis during math and the literature activities during language arts time.

2. These (planned experiences) look hard. I don't think most of my children can do them.

The planned experiences are designed to elicit high abilities and higher level thinking. In field testing, teachers found that most students completed the activities without frustration; however, only a few students exhibited highest levels of achievement. Thus the experiences differentiated for gifted potential as intended.

3. I didn't like a couple of the planned experiences because most of my children didn't do very well.

Of course you care for your children and you want them all to excel. But if all children do equally well on every planned experience, then the activities are not differentiating for the highest ability levels. Remember that, statistically, only a small percentage of children will demonstrate gifted behaviors and produce gifted-level products. Thus, in most cases, only a small number of children in a classroom will produce an outstanding product if a planned experience is to be valid in identifying gifted children.

As a final point, remember that your class will complete only 3 - 6 planned experiences. The rest of your instructional activities will provide many opportunities for all of your children to excel.

4. It takes a lot of time to complete the dictation for kindergarten and first grade children after a planned experience. Is it appropriate for someone to help me take the dictation or must the same person do it all for consistency?

It is definitely appropriate for more than one person to take dictation as long as each person sincerely tries to record the child's ideas using as nearly as possible the child's own words. It is also important that each person prompt the child's response only as suggested in the directions for the planned experience. The suggestions for Taking Dictation from Students (pages 68-70) has several ideas that may help.

5. How much dictation should I take? Are just a few words enough?

Most children will only use a few words to express their ideas. In general, strive to write whatever a child says as long as it is relevant to understanding or interpreting the product.

6. What about my handicapped student who can't complete paper and pencil tests?

During planned experiences, continue any accommodation you typically do for that student in other class assignments. For example, if someone usually takes dictation for that student, do so for the planned experiences also.

7. Some of my children finished a planned experience at different times. What should I do?

The fact that children finish at different times is one more validation of the differences among children. It is appropriate and to be expected that children will vary in the amount of time they spend on an activity.

As individual children finish, use that time to take dictation. Also, allow those finished to go ahead with another activity or independent assignment you have already introduced.

8. Generally, do the sharpest kids get finished first?

Not necessarily. It is always possible that some able children will finish first because they are thinking faster. At other times, a most able child could be one of the last to finish because he/she is working on a more complex solution. Time on task is not always predictive of the quality of the product.

9. What if a student is absent during one of the planned experiences?

It is not absolutely necessary for a child to make up a missed planned experience unless the district has a policy stating that make-ups must be provided. At times, however, a teacher wants a child who was absent to go ahead and complete the missed planned experience because the teacher wants to know how that child will perform. Of course, making up a missed planned experience is recommended if one missed activity would make a difference in a particular child's total results, e.g., one more positive result is needed to meet district norms for inclusion in the gifted program.

10. Do the same kids show up on both the Kingore Observation Inventory (KOI) and the planned experiences?

Usually they do. However, occasionally a child will score high on one and not the other. No single criterion is best for finding all children's talents. Thus, we continue to need to use multiple criteria in gifted identification.

In field testing, teachers suggested that when a student excelled on a planned experience and had not shown up on the KOI, it signaled the teacher to observe carefully to ensure that the child's gifted behaviors were not being overlooked during regular classroom activities. This reconsideration particularly helped the very quiet child who was not speaking out in class but most certainly displayed gifted characteristics in the products being produced.

If a student excelled on the KOI but had not performed well on a planned experience, teachers said that they tried to analyze the situation. Did the students just have an "off day" on the planned experience or had the teacher been over-tallying on KOI observations because the child was a very verbal, outgoing achiever?

11. Our district plans to use the planned experiences every year to provide on-going opportunities to diagnosis children whose abilities emerge at varying times. Won't the children say "We did this last year"?

Yes. The planned experiences are unique enough that most children do remember them. Since the planned experiences have different forms for every grade level, tell the class that these are variations of the activities they did before. Explain that you want them to do the activity because it gives students opportunities to use higher-level thinking. Assure the students that you always want to use activities that allow them to show their best thinking.

Notes & Comments

Planned Experiences Evaluation:

Guidelines
and
Examples

Notes & Comments

Planned Experiences Evaluation: Guidelines & Examples

For each planned experience, a few guidelines and examples are included to assist in the interpretation and scoring. The evaluation guidelines and examples are not intended to be an exhaustive discussion for all possible responses but rather a succinct overview to guide evaluation team members.

A one-page format is used for most of the planned experience making it simple to duplicate and provide to each pair of educators involved in the evaluation process. This format enables districts to easily duplicate only those planned experiences being reviewed by an evaluation team.

In each comment section, the pairs of educators are encouraged to write notes and insights they experience during the evaluation process which might benefit later evaluations of that planned experience. These handwritten notes could be combined and typed on a district or school copy to be distributed next time the planned experiences are used.

Evaluation teams are encouraged to be alert to instances where many students in a class complete a significant part of a planned experience in the same or nearly the same manner. Some child or adult might have influenced that response by modeling the example. In these instances, team members need to decide whether or not gifted behaviors are still being demonstrated by the children.

Characteristics listed in the objectives of each planned experience are the behaviors *most likely* to be elicited. In actuality, any or none of the gifted behaviors may be exhibited as individual children develop a product. Responses always depend on the experiences and abilities of each student.

Educators are encouraged not to be unduly influenced by especially neat or exceptionally messy products. Try to see through the surface appearance to interpret what each product reflects about the gifted potential of a student.

Evaluation: Guidelines & Examples

Title: ☞ <u>Attribute Blocks</u>
☞ <u>Attribute Cards</u>
☞ <u>Attribute Classification</u>

Grades: K, 1, 2-6.

Gifted behaviors demonstrated:

Analytical thinking - Analyzes to include more attributes than typical; attributes may also be more complex or significant.

Perspective - Uses unexpected angle, dimension or point of view.

Accelerated learning - Incorporates attributes which are more abstract or complex than most students' responses. Simultaneously analyzes by multiple attributes.

Advanced language - Uses terminology appropriate to the shapes; vocabulary or syntax may be more advanced or complex than typical.

Criteria demonstrated:

Content - Attributes are more complex or abstract than most students' responses.

Materials - Not applicable in most instances. Building something with the shapes is not the intention of this activity, as that generally distracts students from concentrating on attribute analysis. The opportunity for building with shapes is provided with the Problem Solving with Shapes activity.

Divergence - Unique or clever ideas reflect in-depth understandings; uses several different categories.

Elaboration - Produces a larger number of groups; uses more meaningful detail to explain groups.

Significantly beyond age expectations - Advanced for age of student.

Additional guidelines:

❋ Attribute analysis is the desired outcome of this experience and must be significantly evident to score a "1". Many students will begin creating objects with the shapes when they run out of ideas for analyzing attributes. **Constructions are not to be counted**. Attribute analysis is more abstract; manipulating and constructing objects is more concrete and frequently reflects simpler thinking.

❋ Abstract or complex ideas are more important than just a large number of ideas. For example, a third grader's response of "angles and rounded shapes" was more significant in that class than another child who responded "pretty and not pretty shapes".

❋ By looking over one or more class sets, you will determine the number and types of categories typical of most students in your population. Students who respond in that predictable manner usually scores "W". Students responding with significant categories above that typical number or which are more complex than typical may be scored "1".

✤ Most younger children can only categorize by one attribute at a time. Especially for kindergarten through grade two, then, examples of students simultaneously grouping by two or more categories would score "1".

✤ Field testing found that it was very unusual for students in kindergarten or first grade to understand thickness. Thus, most K-1st children grouping by "thick and thin" score "1".

Comments:

<u>Attribute Blocks</u>

<u>Attribute Cards</u>

<u>Attribute Classification</u>

Evaluation: Guidelines & Examples

Title: ☞ <u>Drawing Starts</u>

Grades: K - 6

Gifted behaviors demonstrated:

Analytical thinking - Analyzes to significantly incorporate a draw start as part of a whole.

Perspective - Drawings or words have unusual angle, dimension or point of view.

Advanced language - Incorporates rich vocabulary or description; syntax may be more complex than typical.

Criteria demonstrated:

Content - The topic or information is advanced, complex or demonstrates more depth than typical.

Materials - Not applicable in most instances. Using the paper in a different position is not considered a resourceful use of materials as it was modeled in the directions.

Organization - Reflects planning in order to incorporate, in a meaningful way, two or more of the figures into one part of the drawing.

Divergence - The idea or the development of the idea is unique or clever.

Elaboration - The drawings or words have detail that especially enriches or clarifies content.

Significantly beyond age expectations - Advanced for age of student.

Additional guidelines:

❀ Any one of the drawings on a page may qualify as indicating gifted behaviors. All of the drawings do not have to be exceptional to score a "1".

❀ A gifted response may be indicated by a drawing, the words explaining a drawing, or both.

Comments:

Evaluation: Guidelines & Examples

Title: ☞ <u>Image Writing</u>

Grades: 2 - 6

Gifted behaviors demonstrated:

Analytical thinking - Plans carefully so words and image compliment one another.

Sensitivity - Words or image reflect unusually sensitive feelings or awareness of another's needs.

Meaning motivation - Both image and words combine to make sense and aid understanding.

Perspective - Feelings may reflect another's point of view; image may involve unusual angle, dimension or viewpoint.

Advanced language - Vocabulary or syntax may be advanced; writing may incorporate a simile, metaphor or analogy to express a relationship.

Criteria demonstrated:

Content - The topic or information is advanced, complex or demonstrates more depth than typical.

Material - Not applicable in most instances.

Organization - To a greater degree, the arrangement shows planning to successfully complete the idea. Volume of writing and size of image are clearly planned to fit together.

Divergence - The words and/or the image are unique or clever or atypical of students in this grade.

Elaboration - The vocabulary is more rich and descriptive than typical; more complex sentence structure than expected. The image has details which enhance and clarify the total product.

Significantly beyond age expectations - Advanced for age of student.

Additional guidelines:

❧ A gifted response may be indicated by the image, the words, or both.

❧ The top of the student handout (the topic to describe) is only intended to guide the student's preparation. It is not considered when scoring the activity. Only the final image and words are evaluated.

Comments:

Evaluation: Guidelines & Examples

Title: ☞ <u>Patterning</u>

Grades: K - 6

Gifted behaviors demonstrated:

Accelerated learning - Pattern is more complex or abstract than most of the other students' responses.

Analytical thinking - Interprets and analyzes the pattern rather than simply repeating it.

Criteria demonstrated:

Content - Pattern is more complex or abstract than most students' responses.

Materials - Not applicable in most instances.

Organization - Reverses a pattern instead of just repeats it; adds another figure to embellish pattern before repeating it.

Divergence - Pattern is unique or more clever than typical. The student's original pattern is especially creative, such as the third grader who made a pattern of seven time-concept words arranged in sequence from "second" to "infinity" and then reversed.

Elaboration - Pattern is complex; details add texture or enrich the pattern more than expected.

Significantly beyond age expectations - Advanced for age of student.

Additional guidelines:

❋ Complex or abstract thinking is more significant here than just being correct.

❋ Most of the students will correctly do some or all of the patterns. A "1", however goes beyond *simple* patterns. A "1" is scored for a product where one or more patterns on the front or back reflect more complexity or seem more difficult than most of the students' responses.

❋ All of the patterns do not have to be correct to score "1". If complex abstract thinking is especially evident in part of the product, it may be scored "1".

❋ In order to be typical of gifted behaviors, the patterns on the back should be original and more complex than most students' responses. The patterns should reflect logic rather than just a list of items. Most students who score "W" draw a simple repetition of two or three figures.

Comments:

Evaluation: Guidelines & Examples

Title: ☞ <u>Problem Solving With Shapes</u>

Grades: K-1 and 2 - 6

Gifted behaviors demonstrated:

Analytical thinking - Plans and organizes carefully; incorporates *all* of the pieces to produce a meaningful whole. May involve a more complex or abstract idea. Presents a logical solution.

Sensitivity - Words reflects unusually sensitive feelings or awareness of the needs of others.

Perspective - Whole or part of the solution involves an unusual angle, dimension or point of view.

Accelerated learning - Successfully incorporates, in a meaningful way, both attributes specified in the directions. Example: "...something found in a hole that helps people in some way." Solution is more complex than typical.

Advanced language - Uses terminology appropriate to the solution but not typical for age. Vocabulary or syntax may be rich or complex.

Criteria demonstrated:

Content - The idea or solution is advanced, complex, or demonstrates more depth than typical.

Materials - Uses the shapes in a different, resourceful manner; may create a 3-dimensional figure such as the fifth grader who made a 3-dimensional wheelchair.

Organization - Incorporates all of the shapes in a meaningful way; more than a random or simple arrangement.

Divergence - Not a common solution; the idea is clever or unique.

Elaboration - Explanation is clearly developed and more descriptive or specific than typical; incorporates more than a basic caption or label. Figure and words go together well.

Significantly beyond age expectations - Advanced for age of student.

Additional guidelines:

❀ Many students will score "W" because they are only able to attend to one attribute instead of successfully incorporating both attributes in their solution. For example, the third grade problem is "Something found at home that helps people in some way." One third grader made a "pet" but did not have any ideas about how the pet could help people.

❀ Solutions which do not incorporate all of the shapes are scored "W". It takes less thinking to only use some of the pieces.

Comments:

Evaluation: Guidelines & Examples

Title: 🖝 <u>Rebus Stories</u>

Grades: K - 6

Gifted behaviors demonstrated:

Analytical thinking - Interprets pictures to produce a more abstract or complex cause and effect relationship. Relates events that occur prior to and after the events suggested in the pictures.

Sense of humor - Plans events for a humorous effect; may use puns or figurative language.

Meaning motivation - Plans carefully so words and pictures compliment each other to produce a meaningful story; continuity of events instead of disjointed events.

Advanced language - Uses terminology appropriate to the pictures and story; vocabulary or syntax may be advanced; writing may incorporate a simile, metaphor or analogy to express a relationship.

Criteria demonstrated:

Content - Incorporates a real sense of story. The topic or information is advanced, complex or demonstrates more depth of meaning than typical. More than a simple listing of the pictures in sequence.

Materials - Uses materials in a different, resourceful manner, e.g., the first grader who glued the pictures along the edge of the paper and then drew an arrow to each picture as it was mentioned in the story.

Organization - Incorporates all of the pictures in a more meaningful manner than typical for most students; logically sequenced. A more clear or unique incorporation of pictures and story.

Divergence - Shows uniqueness of thought; cleverly developed story or clever interpretation of pictures.

Elaboration - Story has rich vocabulary or is more descriptive than typical; involves more than minimal basic facts.

Significantly beyond age expectations - Advanced for age of student.

Additional guidelines:

❀ Most students score "W" because they produce a simple story or even just list the pictures in a sequence.

❀ Evidence of complex or abstract thinking is more significant here than just being able to complete a simple story.

❀ Single or multiple copies of the pictures may be used, but each picture must be incorporated into the story at least once.

Comments:

Evaluation: Guidelines & Examples

Title: ☞ <u>Animals Should Definitely Not Wear Clothing</u>

Grades: 2

Gifted behaviors demonstrated:

Analytical thinking - Plans consequences which fit the initial statement. May involve a more abstract or complex cause and effect relationship instead of typical, simple ideas.

Sense of Humor - Plans events for a humorous effect; may use puns or figurative language. Is funny rather than just silly.

Advanced language - Appropriately uses advanced vocabulary and syntax; more descriptive.

Accelerated learning - Incorporates a concept or consequence that is more advanced or complex than typical, e.g., "Animals should definitely not be paleontologists because they might have to dig up their relatives."

Criteria demonstrated:

Content - The ideas are advanced, complex or demonstrate more depth than typical.

Materials - Uses commonly available materials to add to the effect of the picture. Uses crayons or markers in a less typical way to complete the picture.

Organization - Not applicable in most instances.

Divergence - A very original or creative idea which stands out as unique more than just cute or silly.

Elaboration - The words are descriptive and go beyond minimal statements of "...because they are nice" and "...because they are funny." The picture has details that enhance the total product.

Significantly beyond age expectations - Advanced for age of student.

Additional guidelines:

❀ Most students score "W" because their words or picture are correct yet simple and typical.

❀ Evidence of unique ideas or complex thinking is necessary to score a "1".

❀ A gifted response may be indicated by the complex or humorous words, the picture or both.

Comments:

Evaluation: Guidelines & Examples

Title: ☞ <u>Donna O'Neeshuck was Chased by Some Cows</u>

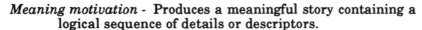

Grades: 4

Gifted behaviors demonstrated:

Analytical thinking - Plans consequences which fit the initial statement. May involve a more abstract idea or a cause and effect relationship instead of more typical, simple ideas.

Meaning motivation - Produces a meaningful story containing a logical sequence of details or descriptors.

Sense of humor - Plans events for a humorous effect; may use puns or figurative language to enhance humor. Is funny rather than just silly.

Sensitivity - The subject, word choices or illustrations reflect unusually sensitive feelings or awareness of self or needs of others.

Advanced language - Appropriately uses advanced vocabulary and syntax; more descriptive than typical. The writing may incorporate a simile, metaphor or analogy to express a relationship. Word choice is purposeful.

Criteria demonstrated:

Content - Incorporates a real sense of story. The subject or information is advanced, complex or demonstrates more depth than typical.

Materials - Not applicable in most instances.

Organization - Incorporates the events in an appropriate but complex manner, such as a circle story that could go on and on.

Divergence - Shows uniqueness of thought; cleverly developed story or clever interpretation of pictures.

Elaboration - The sentences are descriptive and go beyond minimal statements of fact. Extensive detail in words or illustration which adds clarity or effect and is related to content.

Significantly beyond age expectations - Advanced for age of student.

Additional guidelines:

❀ Most students score "W" because their story or pictures are correct yet simple and typical.

❀ Evidence of unique ideas or complex thinking is necessary to score a "1".

❀ A gifted response may be indicated by the complexity or sensitivity of the words, the illustration or both.

❀ Writing in rhyme or not writing in rhyme does not influence the score. The score depends on the quality or complexity of the ideas expressed.

Comments:

Evaluation: Guidelines & Examples

Title: ☞ <u>A House is a House for Me</u>

Grades: 3

Gifted behaviors demonstrated:

Analytical thinking - The analogies are thoughtful and more complex or abstract than typical of most students' responses. Plans pictures to compliment and enhance content.

Perspective - Idea or picture reflects an unexpected point of view, dimension or angle.

Sense of humor - Develops the analogy in an unexpected way for humorous effect, such as "A sneaker is a house for odor." Is funny rather than just silly.

Accelerated language - Expresses a relationship or understanding which is more complex than typical.

Advanced language - Analogies are well developed; uses advanced terminology appropriately to express the relationship.

Criteria demonstrated:

Content - The topic or information is advanced, abstract, complex or demonstrates more depth than typical.

Materials - Not applicable in most instances.

Organization - Not applicable in most instances inasmuch as the pattern for the response has been predetermined.

Divergence - Shows uniqueness of thought; a clever idea. Creative or clever development of pictures. Topic is unusual but appropriate.

Elaboration - The pattern does not encourage much elaboration. Thus, elaboration will mostly be evident in illustrations which add clarity or effect and are related to content.

Significantly beyond age expectations - Advanced for age of student.

Additional guidelines:

❀ Most students score "W" because their statements are correct yet simple and predictable or very much like an idea used in a book.

❀ Evidence of unique ideas or complex thinking is necessary to score a "1".

❀ A gifted response may be indicated by the complexity or humor in the words or picture; but most often it is the combination of both words and picture that produces a gifted response.

❀ Writing in rhyme or not writing in rhyme is not a factor in this evaluation and should not influence the score. The quality of the thinking is the important factor.

Comments:

Evaluation: Guidelines & Examples

Title: ☞ <u>I'm Coming to Get You</u>

Grades: 1

Gifted behaviors demonstrated:

Analytical thinking - The solution is more than a typical, simple idea. It may incorporate a more complex or abstract cause and effect relationship.

Perspective - Student's picture and words demonstrate understanding of the actual small size of the monster. The picture may be drawn from the monster's point of view.

Sense of humor - The student's new episode demonstrates understanding and application of the humor in the original story in which every event also had a funny element. Is funny rather than just silly.

Advanced language - Appropriately uses advanced vocabulary and syntax; more descriptive than typical. Able to use language more effectively than most to explain the situation in the picture.

Criteria demonstrated:

Content - Exhibits in-depth understanding of the main idea of the story.

Materials - Not applicable in most instances.

Organization - Plans the new episode in a more complex manner, such as the child who drew the beginning, middle and end of the episode drawn in three sections from left to right on the paper.

Divergence - A unique, clever idea; creative or clever development of the picture.

Elaboration - The sentences are descriptive and go beyond minimal detail. Extensive detail in sentences or pictures which adds clarity or effect and is related to content.

Significantly beyond age expectations - Advanced for age of student.

Additional guidelines:

✤ Most students score "W" because their stories and pictures show big monsters scaring smaller people and thus indicate they did not comprehend the size concept or main idea of the book.

✤ In the book, the boy was never in a really scary situation. To score "1", then, the new episode should show a small monster and a large boy in a funny situation. For example, one child had a little monster trying to get the boy as he sharpened his pencil; the monster was on the handle of the sharpener and got a whirlwind ride as the boy quickly cranked the handle around and around.

Comments:

Evaluation: Guidelines & Examples

Title: ☞ <u>It Looked Like Spilt Milk</u>

Grades: K

Gifted behaviors demonstrated:

Analytical thinking - Analyzes how to significantly incorporate the picture in a new event for IT LOOKED LIKE SPILT MILK.

Perspective - An unusual angle, dimension or point of view is incorporated in the child's response to the picture.

Sense of humor - Demonstrates a higher-level or finely developed sense of humor; more than just silly.

Advanced language - Incorporates rich vocabulary or description; syntax may be more complex than typical. Able to use language more effectively than most to explain the situation in the picture.

Criteria demonstrated:

Content - Description matches picture well and involves a more complex idea or topic.

Materials - Not applicable in most instances. Using the paper in a different position is not considered a resourceful use of materials as it was modeled in the directions.

Organization - Not applicable in most instances.

Divergence - The idea is unexpected; clever or cleverly developed; shows uniqueness of thought.

Elaboration - The words add details that especially enrich or clarify content.

Significantly beyond age expectations - Advanced for age of student.

Additional guidelines:

❀ Most students score "W" because their ideas are simple and typical.

❀ A "W" is scored when the idea expressed by the words does not clearly relate to the picture.

❀ Evidence of complex and unique thinking are more important here than just a correct but simple match between the words and the picture.

Comments:

Evaluation: Guidelines & Examples

Title: ☞ <u>The Paper Bag Princess</u>

Grades: 6

Gifted behaviors demonstrated:

Advanced language - Appropriately uses advanced vocabulary and syntax; more descriptive than typical. Incorporates analogies to express relationships. Word choice is purposeful.

Analytical thinking - Plans carefully so current events and characters relate to folktale format. Involves a more complex cause and effect relationship. Attempts a dramatic effect or problem resolution.

Sense of humor - Plans events for a humorous effect; more than just silliness. May use puns or figurative language. Is funny rather than just silly.

Sensitivity - Words or pictures reflect unusually sensitive feelings or awareness of the needs of others. Expresses some philosophic or moral theme.

Criteria demonstrated:

Content - The topic or information is advanced, complex or demonstrates more in-depth understanding than typical.

Materials - Uses materials in an appropriate but unexpected manner; resourceful.

Organization - Arranges the events in the story to achieve clarity and best effect. May use a more complex structure, such as a flashback.

Divergence - Approach or content is unlike others of this age; creative ideas or pictures or both. Shows uniqueness of thought; a clever interpretation more than just cute or weird.

Elaboration - The vocabulary is rich and descriptive. Uses many details through words or pictures which enhance and clarify the total story.

Significantly beyond age expectations - Advanced for age of student.

Additional guidelines:

❀ Evidence of complex or abstract thinking is more significant here than just completing a simple or cute story.

❀ Content is more important than mechanics. The story could have mechanical errors and still score a "1".

❀ A gifted response may be indicated by the complexity, humor and sensitivity of the words or the illustration; but most often it is the combination of both words and illustration that produces a gifted response.

Comments:

Evaluation: Guidelines & Examples

Title:  ☞ <u>Q is for Duck</u>

Grades: 1

Gifted behaviors demonstrated:

Analytical thinking - Shared an unusual but appropriate response as the book was read aloud. Produced a more advanced or complex idea in words or picture. Thought of and used more than one word for the letter.

Meaning motivation - Plan carefully so words and pictures compliment each other. Idea makes sense in the context of a classroom.

Sense of humor - Showed understanding of the more subtle humor in the book as it was read aloud. Is funny rather than just silly; may use a pun.

Advanced language - Uses advanced vocabulary or description; syntax may be more complex than typical.

Criteria demonstrated:

Content - Idea is complex or demonstrates more depth than typical.

Materials - Uses materials in a different, resourceful manner.

Organization - A clear and unique incorporation of pictures and words.

Divergence - Clever or unique idea in words or picture; creatively developed.

Elaboration - The vocabulary is more rich and descriptive than typical; more complex sentence structure than expected. Extensive detail in sentence or picture which adds clarity or effect and is related to content.

Significantly beyond age expectations - Advanced for age of student.

Additional guidelines:

✤ Most children will score "W" because they are correct but can only apply a simple, typical response, e.g., A/Apple - "Children in our class like apples." B/Balloon - "Children in our class have balloons."

✤ Some children may score "1" because they use more abstract ideas and adjectives instead of just a simple noun for their letter, e.g., H - "Children in our class are happy HEroes and HERoes."

Comments:

Evaluation: Guidelines & Examples

Title: ☞ <u>The Surprise</u>

Grades: K

Gifted behaviors demonstrated:

Analytical thinking - Planned a more advanced or complex idea in words or pictures. Analyzed how to meet the needs of another and how it could really be accomplished.

Meaning motivation - Both words and pictures combine to make sense and aid understanding.

Sensitivity - Words or picture reflects sensitive feelings or awareness of needs of others to a degree not typical of other students' responses.

Advanced language - Vocabulary or description is more complex than typical. Able to use language more effectively than most to explain the situation in their picture.

Criteria demonstrated:

Content - The idea is advanced or complex; indicates more in-depth understanding of the main idea of the story than typical.

Materials - Uses materials in a different but appropriate manner; resourceful. For example, one child made a pop-up picture to surprise someone.

Organization - The arrangement of the picture is more complex; may show several steps or parts in the whole surprise.

Divergence - Not a common response; the idea or the picture is unique or clever.

Elaboration - Details in the pictures or words enhance and clarify the total product. Provides more than minimum information.

Significantly beyond age expectations - Advanced for age of student.

Additional guidelines:

❀ Evidence of more complex thinking, unique ideas and unusual sensitivity to the needs of others are necessary to score a "1".

❀ Most students score "W" because their words or picture are correct yet simple and typical.

❀ A "W" is scored when the surprise is scary or harmful indicating that the child did not comprehend the main idea of the story of the activity.

Comments:

Evaluation: Guidelines & Examples

Title:  Ten Black Dots

Grades: K

Gifted behaviors demonstrated:

Analytical thinking - Successfully analyzes how to incorporate
all ten dots in a meaningful way in a picture. Produces a
more complex or advanced idea.

Meaning motivation - Plans carefully to incorporate the dots in a picture.
Each dot is a real part of a whole rather than just randomly stuck on.

Perspective - An unusual angle, dimension or point of view is incorporated in a
child's picture or interpretation.

Advanced language - Uses more advanced words or description than typical.
Uses rhymes.

Criteria demonstrated:

Content - The idea is advanced or complex; indicates more in-depth understanding
than typical. For example, one boy put all 10 dopts on top of one another.
He explained that it made a "black hole". The dots had to be on top of each
other to "make the hole deep".

Materials - Uses the materials in a different but appropriate manner; resourceful.

Organization - Plans arrangement so able to incorporate all of the dots
in a logical and appropriate manner.

Divergence - Shows uniqueness of thought; clever incorporation
of dots; creative idea.

Elaboration - Details in words or picture enhance and clarify the total product.

Significantly beyond age expectations - Advanced for age of student.

Additional guidelines:

❀ Evidence of complex and unique thinking are more important
here than just a correct but simple response.

❀ Children may score "1" when they have an especially strong idea and/or
try to incorporate rhyme in their response, as modeled in a book.

❀ Children who are not able to use all ten dots in a significant way
as part of their picture will typically score "W".

❀ Most children score "W" because the response is very simple
or like one suggested in the book.

Comments:

Evaluation: Guidelines & Examples

Title: ☞ <u>Two Bad Ants</u>

Grades: 5

Gifted behaviors demonstrated:

Advanced language - Appropriately uses advanced vocabulary and rich description. Incorporates analogies to express relationships. Word choice is purposeful.

Analytical thinking - Plans a more abstract or complex cause and effect situation. Attempts a dramatic effect or problem resolution.

Perspective - Unusually clever in incorporating ant's needs, feelings or point of view. Pictures involve unusual angle, dimension or point of view.

Sense of humor - Plans events for a humorous effect; more than just silliness. May use puns or figurative language.

Sensitivity - Words or pictures reflect unusually sensitive feelings or awareness of the needs of others. Expresses some philosophic or moral theme.

Criteria demonstrated:

Content - Incorporates ideas that are advanced, complex or demonstrate more in-depth understanding than typical.

Materials - Uses materials in an appropriate but unexpected manner; resourceful.

Organization - Arranges the events in the story to achieve clarity and best effect. May use a more complex structure, such as flashback.

Divergence - Approach or content is unlike others of this age; creative ideas or pictures or both. Shows uniqueness of thought.

Elaboration - The vocabulary is rich and descriptive. Uses many details through words or pictures which enhance and clarify the total story.

Significantly beyond age expectations - Advanced for age of student.

Additional guidelines:

❋   Evidence of complex or abstract thinking is more significant here than just completing a simple or cute story.

❋   Content is more important than mechanics. The story could have mechanical errors and still score a "1".

❋ A gifted response may be indicated by the complexity, humor and unusual sensitivity of the words or illustration; but most often it is the combination of both words and illustration that produces a gifted response.

Comments:

Evaluation: Guidelines & Examples

Title: ☞ <u>What Can You Do with a Pocket?</u>

Grades: 2

Gifted behaviors demonstrated:

Analytical thinking - Analyzes to create clues which are more complex but accurately interpret parts of the whole.

Sense of humor - Plans clues for humorous effect; may use puns or figurative language. Is funny rather than just silly.

Accelerated learning - Clues focus on more complex or abstract attributes than most of the other students' responses.

Meaning motivation - Both picture and words combine to make sense and aid understanding.

Advanced language - Uses terminology appropriate to the picture yet more advanced or descriptive than typical.

Criteria demonstrated:

Content - The ideas are advanced or complex; indicates more in-depth understanding than typical.

Materials - Uses the materials in a different but appropriate manner; resourceful.

Organization - Arranges clues in a logical and appropriate sequence rather than just a random listing.

Divergence - Shows uniqueness of thought; clever clues rather typical ideas; creative.

Elaboration - Details in clues or pictures enhance and clarify the total idea. Clues incorporate more than a simple listing, such as: "It is _____. It has _____. It is _____."

Significantly beyond age expectations - Advanced for age of student.

Additional guidelines:

❀ Most students score "W" because their clues are correct yet simple and typical.

❀ Evidence of in-depth analysis or more complex thinking is necessary to score a "1".

Comments:

Evaluation: Guidelines & Examples

Title: ☞ <u>What's Claude Doing?</u>

Grades: 1

Gifted behaviors demonstrated:

Analytical thinking - Planned a more advanced or complex idea in words or pictures. May incorporate a more complex cause and effect relationship. Analyzed how to help another and figured out how it could really be accomplished.

Advanced language - Vocabulary or description is more complex than typical. Able to use language more effectively than most to explain the idea.

Meaning motivation - Both words and picture combine to make sense and aid understanding.

Sensitivity - Words or picture reflect unusually sensitive feelings or awareness of the needs of others to a degree not typical of other students' responses.

Criteria demonstrated:

Content - The idea is advanced or complex; indicates more in-depth understanding than typical.

Materials - Uses materials in a different but appropriate manner; resourceful.

Organization - A clear and unique incorporation of words and picture; may show several steps or sequence of the child's plan to help another.

Divergence - Not a common response; the idea or picture stands out from the others as unique or clever. Not just a silly, unrealistic idea.

Elaboration - Details in the pictures or words enhance and clarify the total product; provides more than minimum information.

Significantly beyond age expectations - Advanced for age of student.

Additional guidelines:

❋ Most students score "W" because their story or pictures are correct but limited to simple or more typical ideas.

❋ Evidence of unique ideas or complex thinking is necessary to score a "1".

❋ A gifted response may be indicated by the complexity or unusual sensitivity of the words or picture; but most often it is the combination of both words and picture that produces a gifted response.

Comments:

Organizational Chart for Planned Experiences

Advanced Language	Analytical Thinking	Meaning Motivated	Perspective	Sense of Humor	Sensitivity	Accelerated Learning	PLANNED EXPERIENCES	K	1	2	3	4	5	6
X	X					X	Attribute Blocks	118-122						
X	X					X	Attribute Cards		123-127					
X	X		X			X	Attribute Classification			132	133	134	135	136
X	X		X				Drawing Starts	139	140	141	142	143	144	145
X	X	X	X		X		Image Writing			149	150	151	152	153
	X					X	Patterning	156	157	158	159	160	161	162
X	X		X		X	X	Problem Solving With Shapes	165	166	169	170	171	172	173
X	X	X		X			Rebus Stories	178	179	180	181	182	183	184
X	X			X		X	Animals Should Definitely Not Wear Clothing			185-187				
X	X	X		X	X		Donna O'Neeshuck Was Chased By Some Cows					190-191		
X	X		X	X		X	A House Is A House For Me				192-194			
X	X		X	X			I'm Coming To Get You		195, 196					
X	X		X	X			It Looked Like Spilt Milk	197-199						
X	X			X	X		The Paper Bag Princess							200, 201
X	X	X		X			Q Is For Duck		202-204					
X	X	X			X		The Surprise	205						
X	X	X	X				Ten Black Dots	206-208						
X	X		X	X	X		Two Bad Ants						209	
X	X	X		X		X	What Can You Do With A Pocket?			210, 211				
X	X	X			X		What's Claude Doing?		212, 213					

Notes & Comments

Planned Experiences

Copies

of Activities

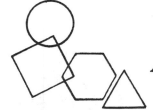

ATTRIBUTE BLOCKS
Evaluation guidelines are on pages 96, 97

Date Due: _____   Teacher: _____

School: _____

Objectives:

1. Student will have an opportunity to use analysis and demonstrate perspective and accelerated learning through the classification of shapes by more than one attribute.

2. Student will have opportunity to use advanced language to explain their classifications.

Materials:

1. Twelve attribute blocks selected to allow classification by color, size, shape,number of sides and thickness. Store them in a self-sealing bag. <u>Note</u>: If plastic attribute blocks are not readily available, the shapes on pages 120, 121 may be used if colored and made thick as stated.

2. Attribute Blocks form - to record class responses, page 122.

Preparing for the Activity:

1. This task should be completed in a one to one setting so children do not see or hear the responses of others.

2. Most students will need about five minutes to complete this activity. A few students with lots of ideas will take longer.

Completing the Activity:

1. Provide the child with the set of 12 blocks. Allow a moment for the child to freely explore and handle the blocks. Do not discuss the colors, shapes cr other attributes of the blocks.

2. Say: *"Use <u>all</u> the blocks; put them into groups that go together."* (Substitute the term *"sort"* or *"categorize"* if the children are more familiar with that word.)

   Allow time for response.
   "Tell me what you did." or *"Why did you put these together?"*

   Record the child's response on the Attribute Block form.

3. Mix up the blocks and encourage the student to regroup them.
   "Is there another way to put these together?"

   Allow time for response.
   "Tell me what you did" or *"Why did you put these together?"*

   Record the child's response on the Attribute Block form.

4. Repeat step 3 as often as the child is able to respond in another way. Continue asking appropriate questions concerning the child's responses.

5. Some children will combine the shapes to build something instead of categorizing by attributues. If that happens, mix up the blocks and say:

"This time, do not try to put the shapes together to make something or build something. Just think about how to sort the shapes into groups that are alike in some way."

If the child again uses the blocks to build something, comment positively on what was made and discontinue the activity.

Recording the Responses:

1. At the completion of each grouping, use the Attribute Block form to check all the ways each child grouped the blocks. For example, check the column under "color" if the child says: "I put all the red ones here and all the blue ones here and the yellow ones here." If the child then regroups the blocks by size, also check "size". If the child forms a grouping which repeats an attribute already demonstrated, encourage the child to think of a completely different way to group the blocks.

2. "Combination of Attributes" is the column to use if a child *simultaneously* groups by more than one attribute. For example, "These are small, red blocks." Make a note under "Combinations" listing the two or more attributes the child used. Most children will not group by two or more attributes.

3. "Other" is the response to check if the student's grouping is an appropriate classification but doesn't fit the categories listed. Briefly list the way the student grouped the blocks. Note any other interesting observations which provide insight into the child's thinking.

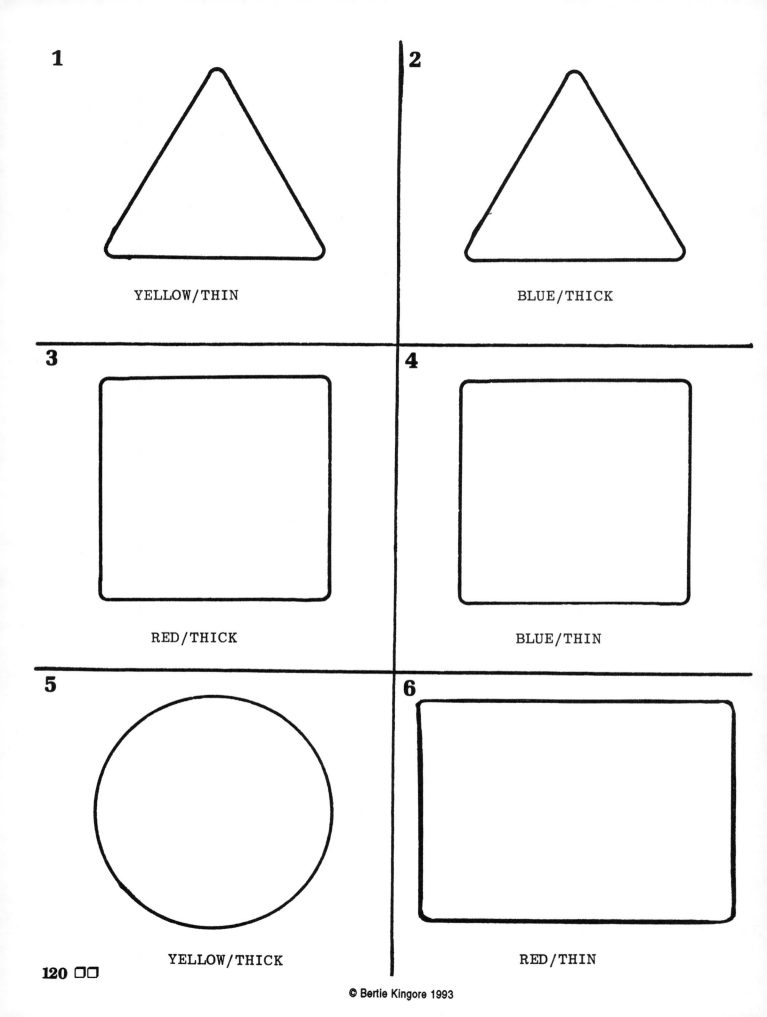

1

YELLOW/THIN

2

BLUE/THICK

3

RED/THICK

4

BLUE/THIN

5

YELLOW/THICK

6

RED/THIN

7

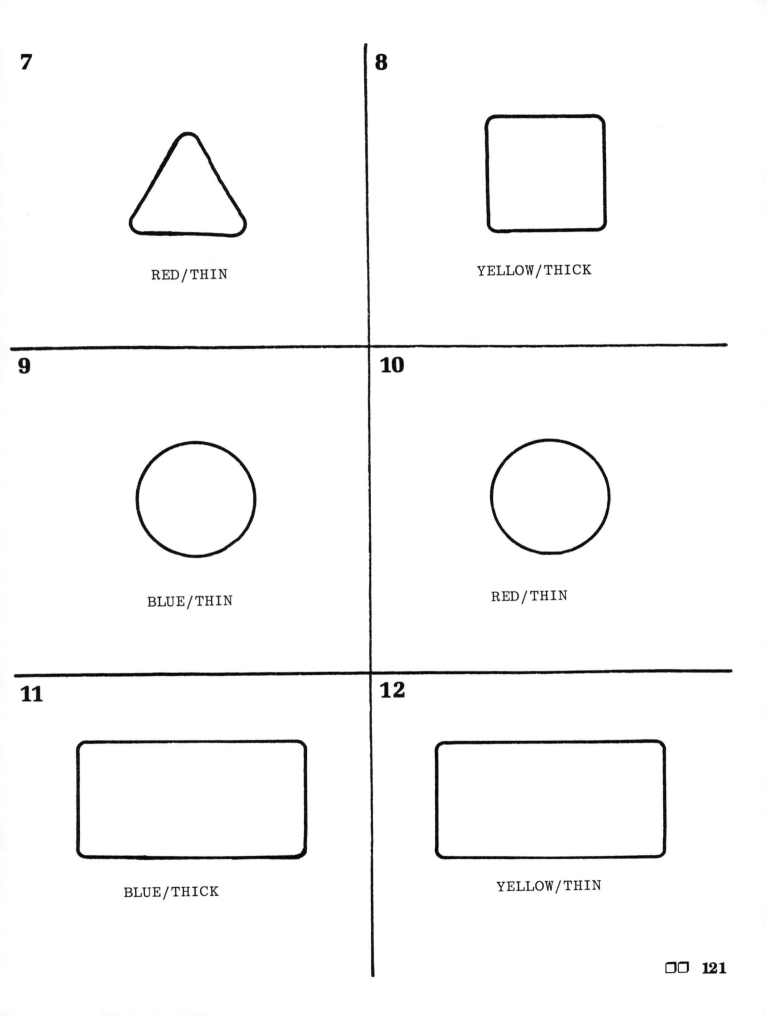

RED/THIN

8

YELLOW/THICK

9

BLUE/THIN

10

RED/THIN

11

BLUE/THICK

12

YELLOW/THIN

ATTRIBUTE BLOCKS

Names	Color	Size	Shape	Thickness	Number of Sides	Combinations of Attributes	Other/Comments	Score

ATTRIBUTE CARDS
Evaluation guidelines are on pages 96, 97

Date due:_____   Teacher: _____

School: _____

Objectives:

1. Student will have an opportunity to use analysis and demonstrate perspective and accelerated learning through the classification of shapes by more than one attribute.

2. Student will have opportunity to use advanced language to explain their classifications.

Materials:

1. Twelve attribute cards are selected to allow classification by shape, size, multiple shapes and shapes within shapes. Store them in a self-sealing bag.

2. Attribute Card form (page 127) to record class responses.

Preparing for the Activity:

1. This task should be completed in a one to one setting so children do not see or hear the responses of others.

2. Most students will need about five minutes to complete this activity.

Completing the Activity:

1. Allow a moment for the student to examine and handle the cards. Do not discuss the color, shapes, or other attributes of the cards.

2. Say: "Use <u>all</u> the cards; put them into groups that go together."
(Substitute the term "sort" or "categorize" if the children are more familiar with that word.)

     Allow time for response.

   "Tell me what you did." or *"Why did you put these together?"*

     Record the student's responses on the Attribute Card form.

3. Mix up the cards and encourage the student to regroup them.

   "Is there another way to put these together?"

     Allow time for response.

   "Tell me what you did." or *"Why did you put these together?"*

     Record the child's response on the Attribute Card form.

4. Repeat step 3 as often as the student is able to respond in another way. Continue asking appropriate questions concerning the student's responses.

5. Some children will combine the shapes to build something instead of categorizing by attributes. If that happens, mix up the cards and say:

"This time, do not try to put the shapes together to makes something or build something. Just think about how to sort the shapes into groups that are alike in some way."

If the child again uses the cards to build something, comment positively on what was made and discontinue the activity.

Recording the Activity:

1. At the completion of each grouping, use the Attribute Card form to check all the ways a student grouped the blocks. For example, check the column under "shape" if a student says: "I put all the rectangles here, all the squares here, the circles here, and the hexagons here." If the student then regroups the blocks by size, also check "size". If the student forms a grouping which repeats an attribute already demonstrated, encourage the child to think of a completely different way to group the blocks.

2. "Combination of Attributes" is the column to use if a student *simultaneously* groups by more than one attribute. For example, "These are small circles in groups." Make a note under "Combination" listing the two or more attributes the child used.

3. "Other" is the response to check if the student's grouping is an appropriate classification but doesn't fit the categories listed. Briefly list the way the student grouped the blocks. Note any other interesting observations which provide insight into the student's thinking.

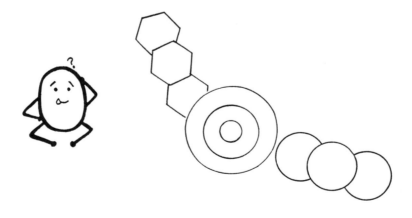

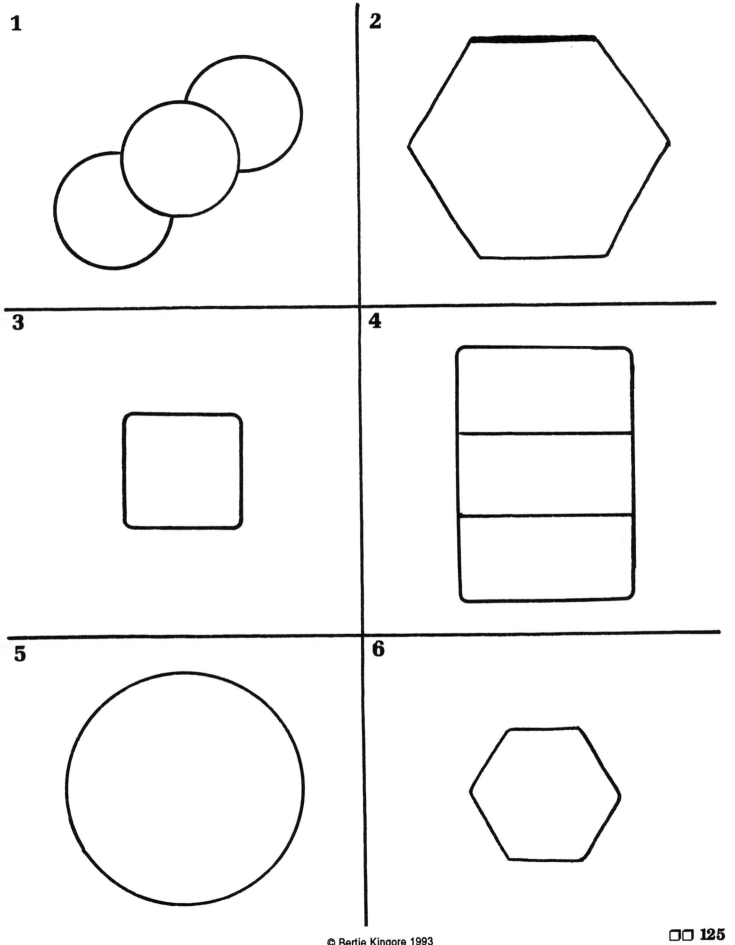

1

2

3

4

5

6

125

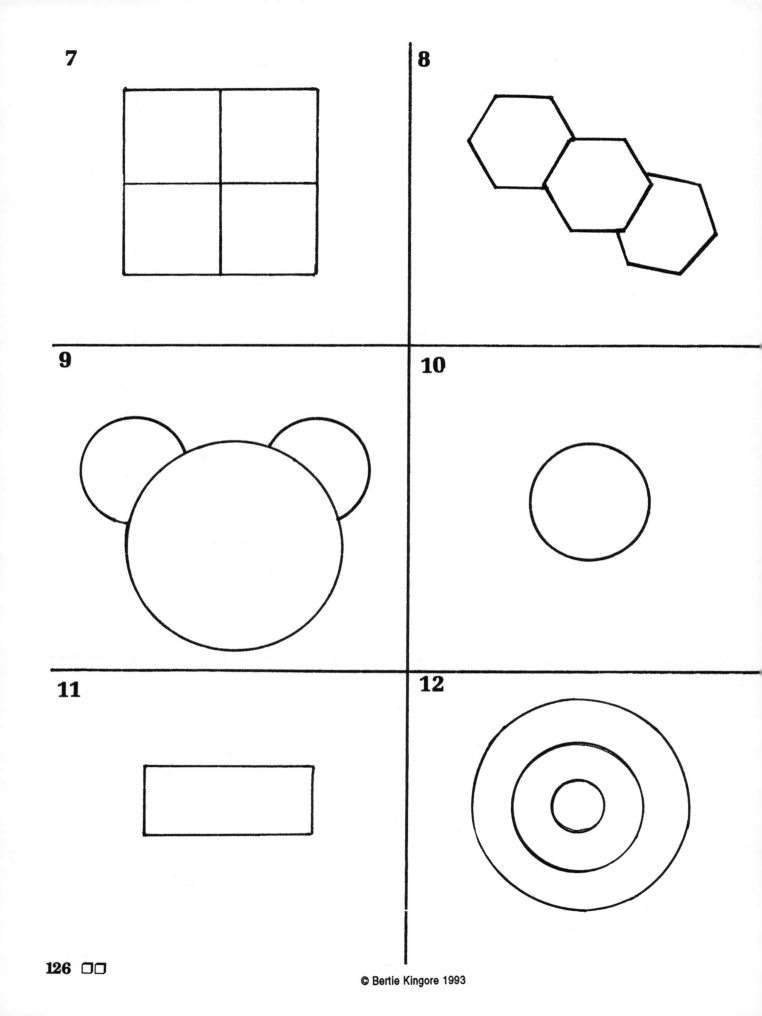

ATTRIBUTE CARDS

Names	Shapes	Size	Multiple Shapes	Shapes Within Shapes	Combinations of Attributes	Other/Comments	Score

ATTRIBUTE CLASSIFICATIONS

Evaluation guidelines are on pages 96, 97

Date: _____   Teacher: _____

School: _____

Objectives:

1. Students will have an opportunity to use analysis and demonstrate perspective and accelerated learning through the classification of shapes by multiple attributes.

2. Students will have an opportunity to use advanced language to explain their classifications.

Materials:

1. Introduction Shapes, page 130.

2. Optional: Overhead transparency of Introduction Shapes.

3. Shape handout designated for each grade level.

4. Shape Classification form, page 131.

5. Pen or pencil.

Preparing for the Activity:

1. To demonstrate the activity on the chalkboard, cut apart the Introduction Shapes and use loops of masking tape on each shape so it will adhere to the chalkboard. To demonstrate the activity on an overhead, cut apart a transparency of the Introduction Shapes.

2. This activity is untimed and may be administered in whole class, small groups or individual settings. Most students will need approximately 10 - 15 minutes to complete this activity. This time estimate does not include cutting out the shapes as that is optional. Teachers may explain all of the directions and allow students to proceed independently until they are finished. Thus, this activity works well during that part of the day when children are scheduled to complete independent seat work.

2. Encourage individual responses or arrange for individual work spaces. (See Suggestions for Encouraging Individuality on page 67.)

Demonstrating the Activity:

Using the Introduction Shapes, say:

"Look at these shapes and think about ways you could put some or even all of these shapes together in a group. For example, shapes B, I and K could go together because they are triangles. On this Shape Classification page (hold up handout), we would write the three alphabet letters of these shapes under "Groups" and then write why they go together on these lines beside the group." (Demonstrate)

"Sometimes there are many reasons shapes go together. Think for a minute. Tell me any other reason you can think of for why these three shapes we've listed as a group go together."

(Write on the Shape Classification additional ideas for that group, such as all are three-sided.)

"Now, let's look at the whole page of shapes again. Using the same or different ones, using any number of the shapes that you want to, find another group and name these letters for the class. Tell us why they go together." (Allow time for one or two responses.)

"Tell me another reason these go together."

(Encourage additional ideas.).

Completing the activity:

1. Provide each student with the Shapes Classification form and the Shape handout appropriate for that grade level. (Grade level indicated on each page beside the copyright symbol.) Make sure the students put their names on the back of the Shape Classification form. Students may cut apart the shapes on the Shape handout so they may move them around and make groups more easily, or they may leave the Shape handout intact and just visualize which shapes may be grouped.

2. Read aloud to the students the directions of the Shape Classification handout. Then say:

   "There is room on this page for a lot of different groups. Think of as many different groups as you can; but you certainly don't have to fill up all the lines. If you need more room, you may also write on the back of the paper. For each group you make, try to think of many ways they go together."

   "Do not try to make pictures or objects by combining the shapes. Rather, think about the attributes or characteristics of each shape and how some shapes might to together and be grouped in the same way."

3. Make a note of students who analyze successfully by visualizing the groupings without manipulating the shapes. That approach is related to learning style but may also provide clues to abstract or complex thinking.

INTRODUCTORY SHAPES

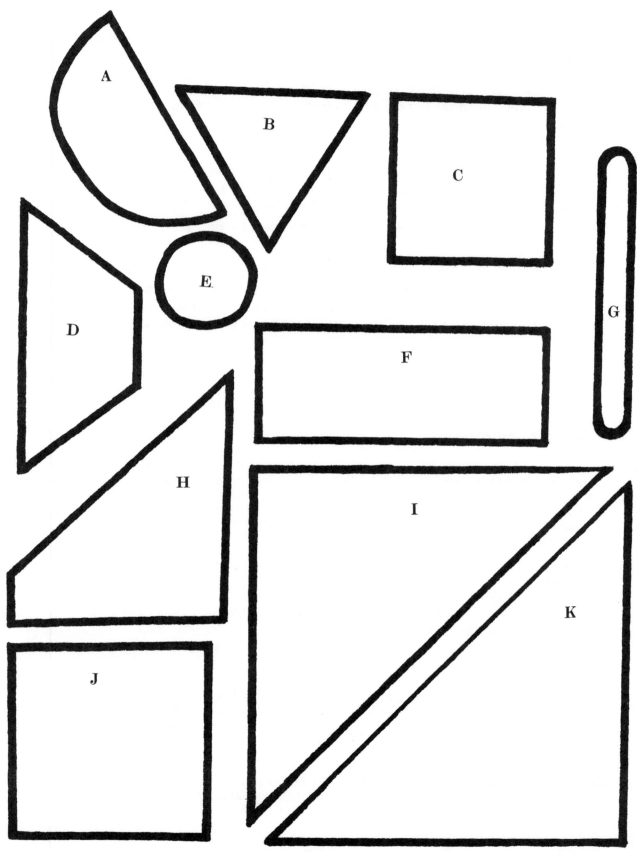

SHAPE CLASSIFICATION

Think about ways to group any or all of these shapes. List the letters of the shapes that go together in some way and write a few words to explain all the different ways they belong together. Keep thinking about other ways to group the shapes and list as many different groups as you can. Try to think of common groups and also lots of groups that no one else will think of. Use the back of the page to list more groups if you need room.

GROUPS   **WHY DO THEY GO TOGETHER?**

1.

2.

3.

4.

5.

6.

7.

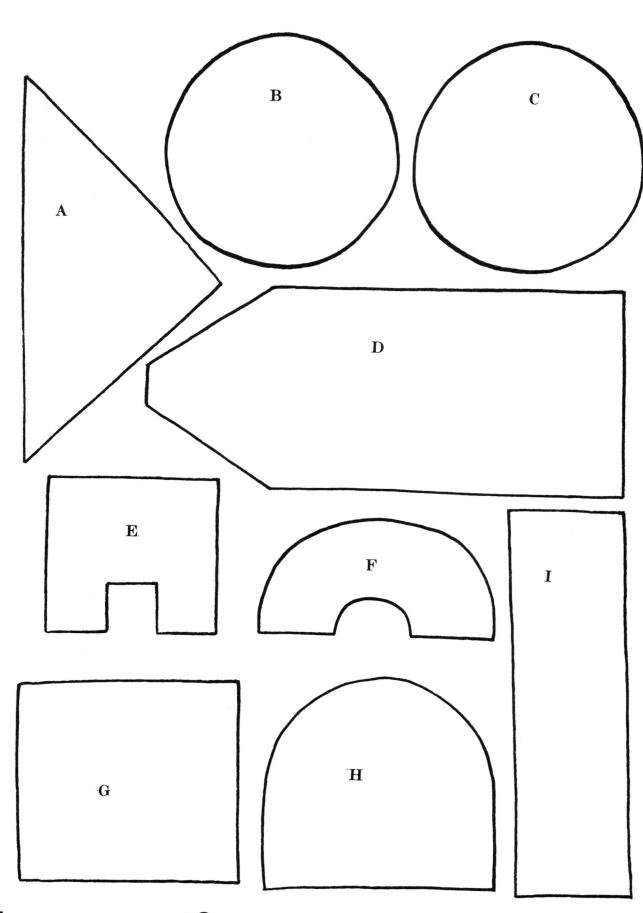

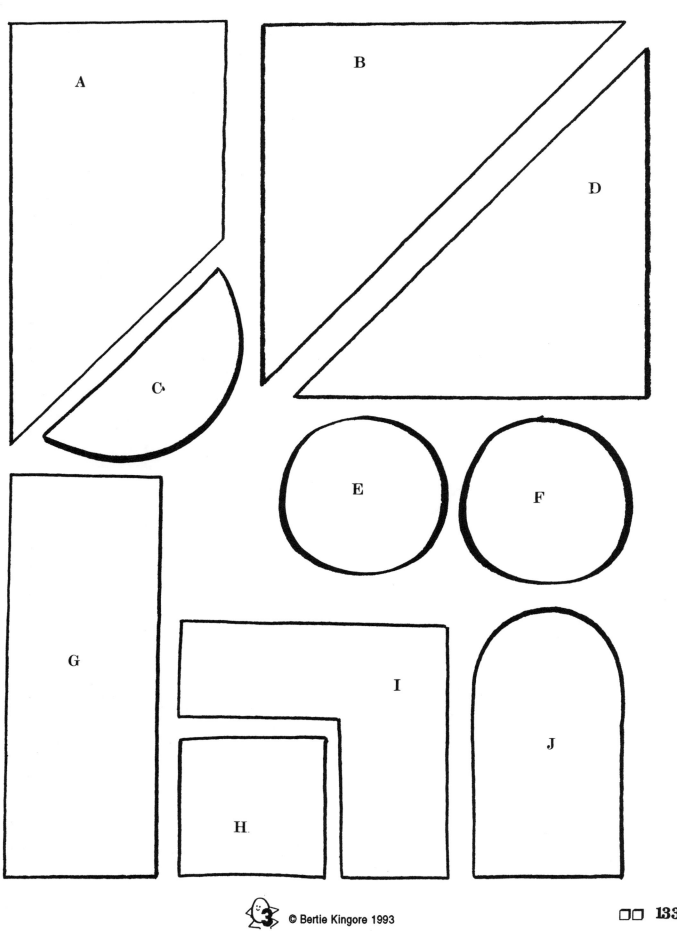

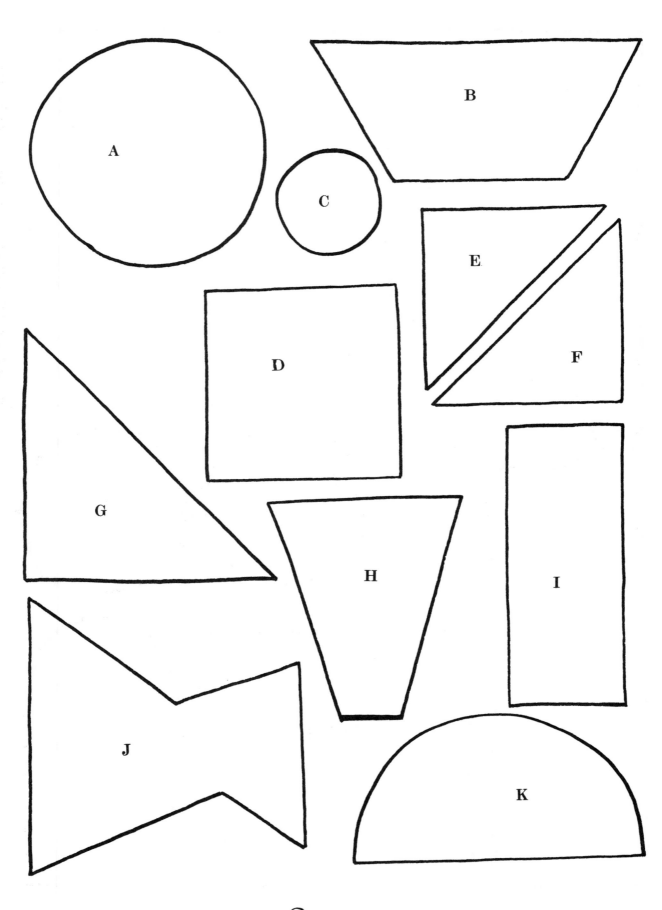

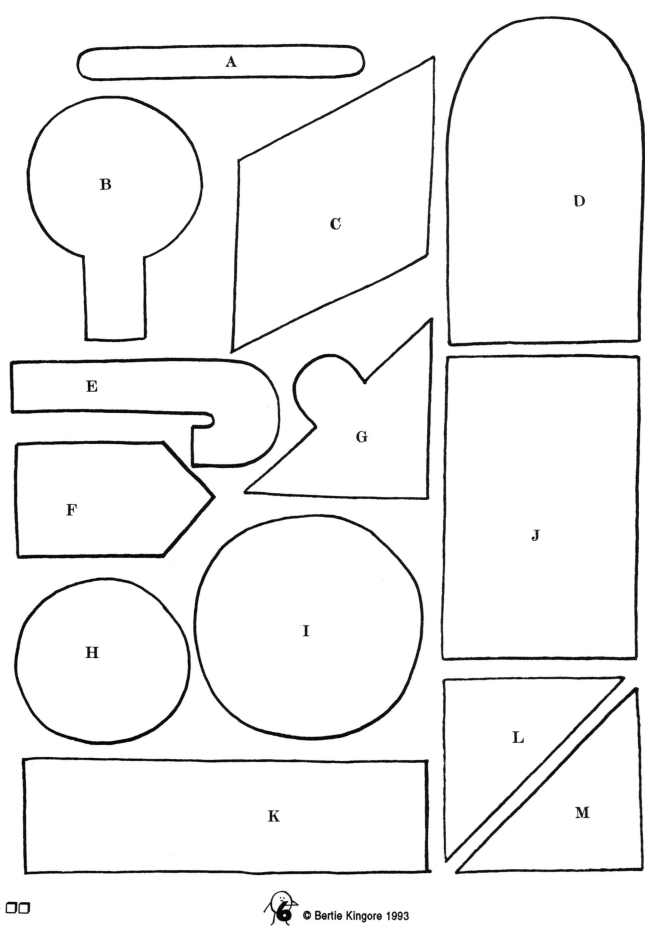

DRAWING STARTS
Evaluation guidelines are on page 98

Date due: _____   Teacher:_____

School: _____

Objectives:

1. Students will have an opportunity to use perspective and analysis to complete two to four incomplete figures.

2. Students will have an opportunity to use advanced language to explain their thinking and write or tell about their completed drawings.

Materials:

Drawing Starts handout appropriate to grade level

Pencils

Preparing for the Activity:

1. This activity is untimed and may be administered in whole group, small groups or individual settings. Most students complete the activity in just 5-10 minutes. But some children will take longer because of the thinking and planning they are doing.

2. Encourage individuality (see Suggestions for Encouraging Individuality on page 67) or arrange student's working space out of the view of others.

3. Provide only pencils for drawing. During field testing, students were found to add more detail and elaboration when using pencils rather than crayons. When using crayons or markers, some children became more interested in coloring the figures and lost their concentration and complexity of writing.

4. The student or teacher writes the student's name on the back of the handout.

Completing the Activity:

1. Hand out the student's copy of the handout.

2. Say to each student:

   "Look at the drawings on this page. These drawings aren't finished yet but there are lots of things they could be. Think about what they could be. Try to think of an idea no one else might think of. Use your imagination and make the drawings into something. You may draw it with your paper like this or like this or like this or this."

   As you talk, hold the handout and rotate it one turn clockwise each time to accent drawing with their paper in any position.

   "After you finish your drawing, I want you to write or tell me about it. Use a pencil and finish your drawing now."

3. Most students will draw separate figures for each of the drawing starts. Occasionally, a student may combine two or more figures into one drawing. That is certainly permissible and often very exciting. However, avoid suggesting that students combine the figures in their drawings, thus allowing children to discover that possibility for themselves.

4. After the drawings are complete, either remind each student to write an explanation for each drawing or ask each student *individually* to tell you about the drawings. (See Suggestions for Taking Dictation on pages 68-70.)

   Say to each student:

   "Write or tell me all about your drawings."

   If more explanation is desired, say:

   "Write or tell me some more to help me understand your thinking."

   A brief explanation is needed beside each drawing, using as many of the child's words as possible, in order that adults may better understand the insights and depth of the student's thinking. For example, the student might:
   a) simply name the objects drawn,
   b) tell a sentence or sentences about the drawing,
   c) tell a brief story, or
   d) relate a scenario connecting more than one of the drawings.

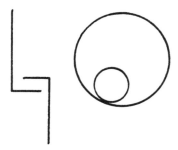

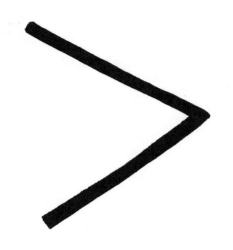

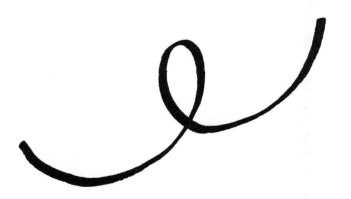

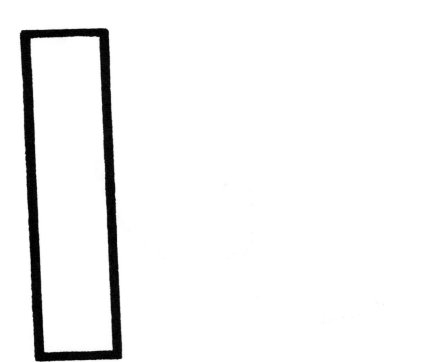

□□

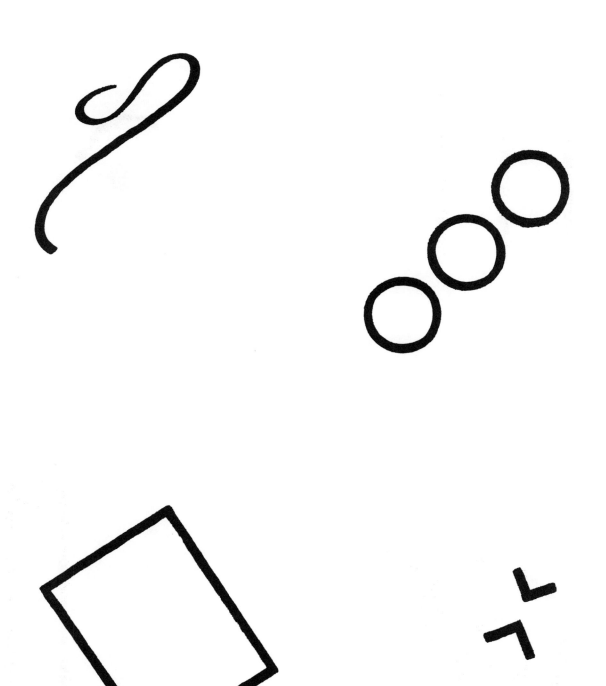

IMAGE WRITING
Evaluation guidelines are on page 99

Date due: _____   Teacher: _____

School: _____

Objective:

Students will have an opportunity to use analytical thinking, sensitivity, meaning motivation, perspective and advanced language to complete an image writing.

Materials: Image Writing handout - appropriate to grade level

Kite writing, page 148

Pencils

Crayons or markers

Optional: Shel Silverstein's book: <u>Where the Sidewalk Ends</u>

Preparing for the Activity:

1. This activity is untimed and may be administered to whole group, small groups or individual settings. Most students will complete this activity in about twenty-five minutes.

2. Encourage individuality or arrange students' working space out of the view of others (See Suggestions for Encouraging Individuality on page 67.)

3. If available, read and show the children the giraffe poem (page 107) and the Miss Betsy Blue Bonnet poem (pages 134-135) of Shel Silverstein's <u>Where the Sidewalk Ends</u> as additional examples of sentences written as an image of their subjects.

4. Students are welcomes to use a dictionary, thesaurus or other sources if you wish to provide that opportunity for all students.

Demonstrating the Activity:

1. Say to the students:

"Instead of just writing regular sentences, some writers arrange their words to create a picture or an image of their idea. We call this kind of writing image writing because the words make a picture or an image of the subject. Here are two sentences about a kite. Look how they've been written to look like a kite." (Show picture or overhead of the kite.)

2. Next say:

"Image writing doesn't have to rhyme. Tell me a sentence about a large ball we could play with outside."

Get ideas about the ball from the students. On the chalkboard, write one or more sentences about the ball. Encourage the use of interesting words and ideas.

"Now how could I arrange these words to create an image or picture?"

Students will probably suggest writing the sentence(s) in a circle to look like a ball. Quickly rewrite the sentence(s) in the image they suggest. Draw an arrow to show where the image writing begins.

Completing the Activity:

1. Provide the students with a copy of the appropriate grade-level handout and say:

"Here is a paper for you to complete your own image writing. Think hard and try to think of an idea that no one else might think of. Then complete your image writing. You may add details with your pencil or crayons if you wish."

Read the directions on the handout to the students, if desired.

2. Teachers may explain all of the directions and allow the students to work independently as long as they need. Thus, this activity works well during that part of the day when students are scheduled to complete independent seat work.

Fly
and soar
dip and dive
chase the wind
as if alive
The dancing
kite can
float
and
fly
until
it seems to touch the sky.

Anonymous

Image Writing

Directions: List as many words as you can to tell your ideas and feelings about any or all of the following topics. Try to think of unusual and interesting words to describe the topic.

dinosaur _____

_____

clown _____

_____

favorite animal _____

_____

eating _____

_____

Example:
Image-writing
about a flower

Image-writing about a flower: I think I'll watch and see. I wonder how it feels to be alone at night... This flower is a lovely sight. It makes the day seem beautiful and bright.

Directions: Write several sentences about <u>one</u> of the above topics. Use the best words and ideas you thought of about that topic. Make your image writing tell how the object feels or how you feel about the object.

_____

_____

_____

_____

_____

Directions:
1. Now think of the best shape to go with your ideas.
2. On the back, or on another sheet of paper, write your sentences into the shape of an image or picture to complete your image writing.
3. Draw an arrow to show where your image writing begins.

Image Writing

Directions: *List as many words as you can to tell your ideas and feelings about any or all of the following topics.   Try to think of unusual and interesting words to describe the topic.*

roller coaster _____

_____

trees _____

_____

soccer _____

_____

playing _____

_____

The image writing example (spiral text about a flower) reads: I think I'll be alone at night . . . I wonder how it feels to be alone at night. I'll watch and see. I wonder how it feels. This flower is a lovely sight. It makes the day seem beautiful and bright.

Example:
Image-writing
about a flower

Directions: *Write several sentences about <u>one</u> of the above topics.   Use the best words and ideas you thought of about that topic.   Make your image writing tell how the object feels or how you feel about the object.*

_____

_____

_____

_____

_____

Directions:
1. Now think of the best shape to go with your ideas.
2. On the back, or on another sheet of paper, write your sentences
    into the shape of an image or picture to complete your image writing.
3. Draw an arrow to show where your image writing begins.

Image Writing

Directions: List as many words as you can to tell your ideas and feelings
about any or all of the following topics. Try to think of unusual
and interesting words to describe the topic.

video games _____

_____

birds _____

_____

trains _____

_____

watching television _____

_____

Example:
Image-writing
about a flower

Directions: Write several sentences about <u>one</u> of the above topics. Use the
best words and ideas you thought of about that topic. Make your image
writing tell how the object feels or how you feel about the object.

_____

_____

_____

_____

_____

Directions:
1. Now think of the best shape to go with your ideas.
2. On the back, or on another sheet of paper, write your sentences
    into the shape of an image or picture to complete your image writing.
3. Draw an arrow to show where your image writing begins.

© Bertie Kingore 1993

151

Image Writing

Directions: *List as many words as you can to tell your ideas and feelings about any or all of the following topics. Try to think of unusual and interesting words to describe the topic.*

space shuttle _____

_____

waterfalls _____

_____

baseball _____

_____

traveling _____

_____

(Image-writing about a flower, arranged in flower shape:) I think I'll watch and see... I'll be alone at night. I wonder how it feels to be alone at night. This flower is a lovely sight. It makes the day seem beautiful and bright.

Example:
Image-writing
about a flower

Directions: *Write several sentences about <u>one</u> of the above topics. Use the best words and ideas you thought of about that topic. Make your image writing tell how the object feels or how you feel about the object.*

_____

_____

_____

_____

_____

Directions:
1. *Now think of the best shape to go with your ideas.*
2. *On the back, or on another sheet of paper, write your sentences into the shape of an image or picture to complete your image writing.*
3. *Draw an arrow to show where your image writing begins.*

Image Writing

Directions: *List as many words as you can to tell your ideas and feelings about any or all of the following topics. Try to think of unusual and interesting words to describe the topic.*

computer _____

_____

butterflies _____

_____

football _____

_____

shopping _____

_____

Example:
Image-writing
about a flower

Directions: *Write several sentences about __one__ of the above topics. Use the best words and ideas you thought of about that topic. Make your image writing tell how the object feels or how you feel about the object.*

_____

_____

_____

_____

_____

Directions:
1. Now think of the best shape to go with your ideas.
2. On the back, or on another sheet of paper, write your sentences into the shape of an image or picture to complete your image writing.
3. Draw an arrow to show where your image writing begins.

PATTERNING
Evaluation guidelines are on page 100

Date due: _____   Teacher: _____

School: _____

Objective:

Student will have an opportunity to demonstrate accelerated learning and analytical thinking by completing and creating patterns.

Materials:

Patterns handout appropriate to grade level

Pencils or crayons

Preparing for the Activity:

1. This activity is untimed and may be administered in whole class, small groups, or individual settings. Most students will complete this activity in five to ten minutes. Some students will take longer, especially if they are creating more complex patterns.

2. Encourage individual responses or arrange for individual work spaces. (See Suggestions for Encouraging Individuality on page 67)

Demonstrating the Activity:

1. On the chalkboard, draw this example:

"I've drawn a pattern here. What do you think the next shape should be? Tell me what to draw to finish the pattern."

Let the children take turns either drawing the next shape, or telling you what to draw. Ask them to explain why that shape goes there. Note any children who demonstrate unusual analytical reasoning in their responses.

2. Next, draw this pattern and repeat the process above.

3. Then, write these numbers on the board.

1, 2, 3, 4

"Sometimes a pattern keeps developing in different ways. (For younger children, touch each numeral as you say it.) *This is one, two, three, four, Tell me what to write next in this pattern."*

After the children respond ask:

Is there an another way to complete this pattern?"

Note any children whose answers extend beyond typical responses.

4. Finally, draw this pattern in the *middle* of the board.

"Sometimes we can draw on both ends of a pattern. (For younger children, touch each shape as you say it.) *This is a circle, triangle, circle, triangle. Tell me what to draw next.* (Touch the space to the *right* of the last triangle. After drawing what the children tell you, touch the space to the *left* of the first circle.) *Now tell me what to draw here."*

Completing the Activity:

1. Distribute the handout. Make sure the children put their names on their paper.

2. Say to the students:

"Finish the patterns. Draw what you think should come next in each part of a pattern. Think carefully. You might even think of a really difficult pattern. When you finish, turn your paper over and make your own patterns on the back. Try to make a complex pattern. Try to make a pattern no one else has done."

If children finish the front of the paper and forget to turn their paper over, it is appropriate to remind them by repeating the last three sentences in the above directions.

3. This activity allows children the opportunity to repeat patterns and complete patterns in more complex ways. Many children will only be able to form simple instead of complex patterns. Whatever the children do, if the teacher is accepting, they gennerally feel successful. If a child gets confused or stumped, gently encourage him/her:

"Just finish the patterns any way you can. Your ideas are important."

4. If a child only adds one figure to any row and you think he/she can successfully do more, ask him/her:

"Make one more in each row." or *"Go ahead and finish each row."*

When a child adds just one figure to the printed pattern it is often more difficult to interpret the level of the child's thinking about each pattern.

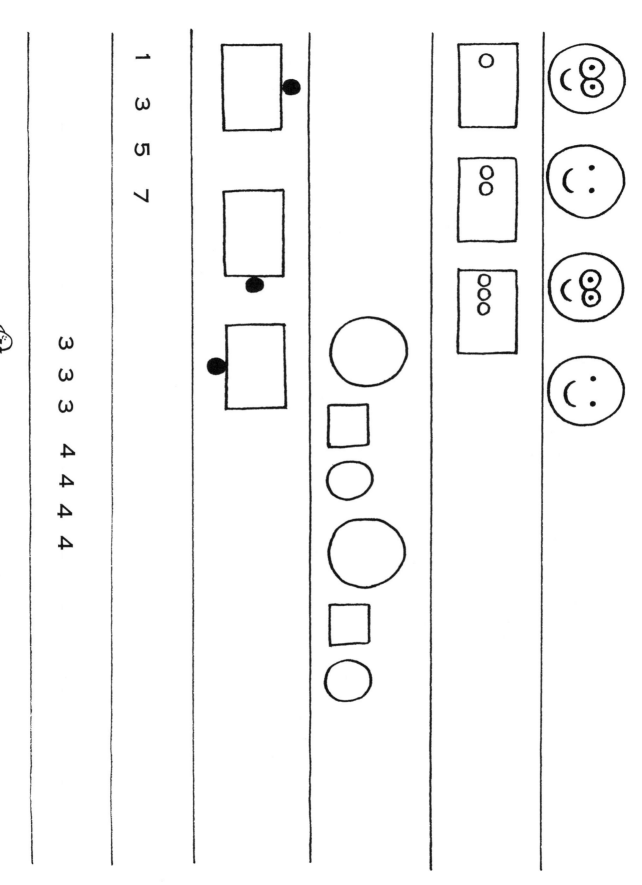

1   3   5   7

3   3   4   4   4

1A 2B 3C

11 9 7 5

3 6 9

54321   4321   321

E G I

X XX XXX X/XXX

21 17 13 9

0 1 2 4 5 6

159

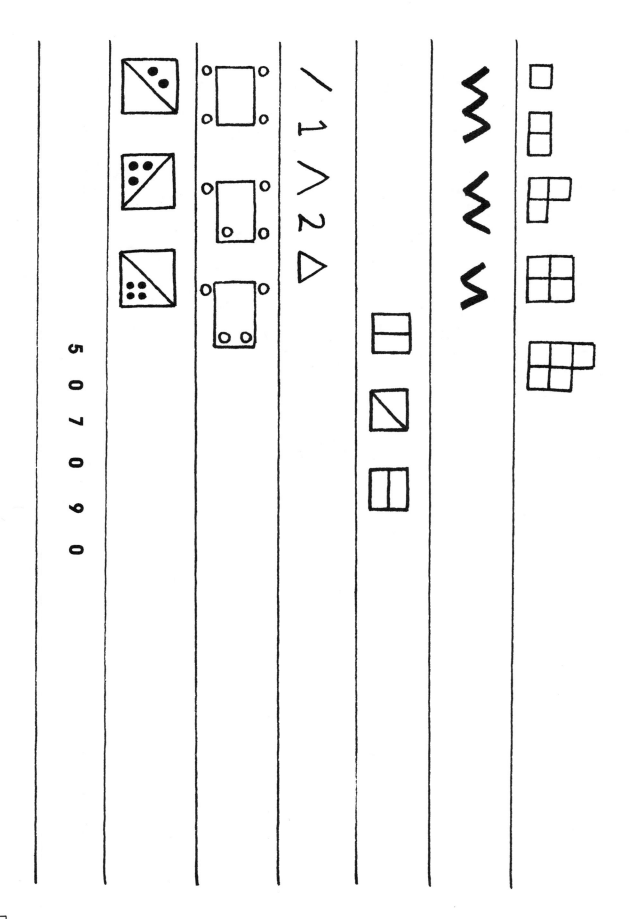

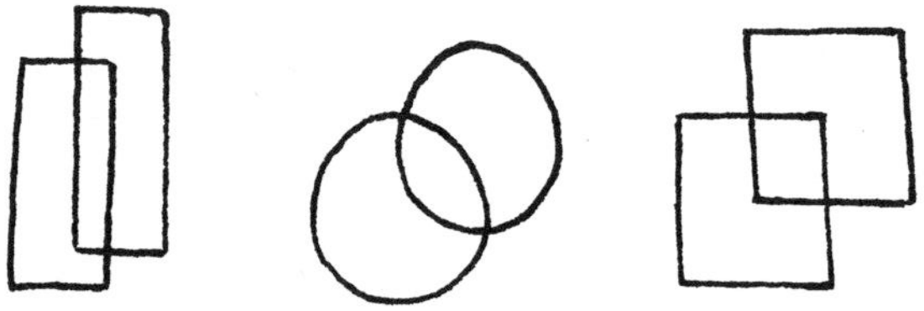

3 △ 4 □ 5 ⬠

4 8 16

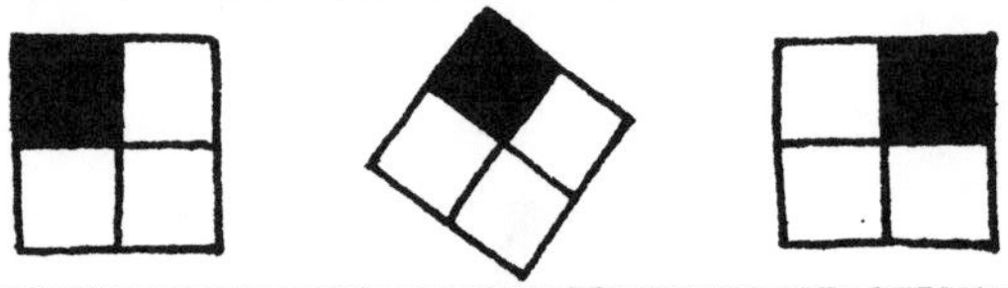

0 3 2 5 4

an   ban   can

ZXW   USR   PNM

H A

PROBLEM SOLVING WITH SHAPES

Evaluation guidelines are on page 101

Date due: _____   Teacher: _____

                                School: _____

Objectives:

1. Students will have an opportunity to use analysis, perspective and demonstrate sensitivity through the organization of shapes to solve a problem.

2. Students will have an opportunity to demonstrate accelerated learning by successfully incorporating both attributes of the problem in their solution.

3. Students will have an opportunity to use advanced language to explain their solution.

Materials:

1. Shape handout appropriate to grade level
2. Scissors
3. Paper
4. Pen or pencil
5. Glue

Preparing for the Activity:

1. This activity is untimed and may be administered in whole class, small groups or individual settings. Most students will need twenty to twenty-five minutes to cut out the shapes and complete this activity. Teachers may explain all of the directions and allow students to proceed independently until they are finished. Thus, this activity works well during that part of the day when children are scheduled to complete independent seat work.

2. Encourage individual responses or arrange for individual work spaces. (See Suggestions for Encouraging Individuality on page 67)

3. It is best not to provide glue too quickly during this activity. Encourage the children to explore several ideas by moving shapes around until they have their best idea. Then they should get the glue. If glue is provided at the beginning of the activity, some young children glue the shapes down with less thought.

Completing the Activity:

1. Provide each student with the appropriate Shapes handout.

2. Say:

   "Cut out each shape on this paper (hold up handout) *so you can use the shapes to solve a problem. After they are cut out, look at them and think about them. Move them around and think about how they could go together to...*
   (Read only the one problem below which is appropriate to the students' grade level.)

Grade	Problem
Kindergarten	*"...make something that can move around and helps people in some way."*
First	*"...make something that makes a sound or noise and helps people in some way."*

   "You need to use all the shapes. You may not cut them to make them smaller."

   "There are lots of different ways to use the shapes to solve the problem. Keep thinking until you have a really good idea. When you have thought of your best idea, get some glue and glue the shapes on your paper the way you want them to go together."

3. As students finish, either invite them to write on their paper to explain their solution or ask each one individually:

   "Tell me what you have made."

Grade	Question
Kindergarten	*"How does it move around and help people?"*
First	*"How does it make a sound or noise and help people?"*

   If more explanation is desired, say:

   "Tell me some more to help me understand your thinking."

   (See Suggestions for Taking Dictation on page 68-70). Write a brief explanation on the child's paper using as many of the child's actual words as possible.

4. Depending on their stage of development, some young children are only able to attend to one attribute of the problem. For example, when asked to make something that can move around and helps people in some way, some children created something that moved but they did not also figure out how it helped people.

5. Occasionally, a child will want to use a pencil or crayons to add details. It is appropriate for children to do so after they have glued the shapes to show their best idea.

6. If needed or desired, the shapes may be cut out for a child since a child's ability to solve this problem should not be hampered by difficulties with fine motor coordination.

PROBLEM SOLVING WITH SHAPES
Evaluation guidelines are on page 101

Date due: _____   Teacher: _____

School: _____

Objectives:

1. Students will have an opportunity to use analysis, perspective and demonstrate sensitivity through the organization of shapes to solve a problem.

2. Students will have an opportunity to demonstrate accelerated learning by successfully incorporating both attributes of the problem in their solution.

3. Students will have an opportunity to use advanced language to explain their solution.

Materials:

1. Shape handout appropriate to grade level
2. Scissors
3. Paper
4. Pen or pencil
5. Glue

Preparing for the Activity:

1. This activity is untimed and may be administered in whole class, small groups or individual settings. Most students will need twenty to twenty-five minutes to cut out the shapes and complete this activity. Teachers may explain all of the directions and allow students to proceed independently until they are finished. Thus, this activity works well during that part of the day when children are scheduled to complete independent seat work.

2. Encourage individual responses or arrange for individual work spaces. (See Suggestions for Encouraging Individuality on page 67.)

3. It is best not to provide glue too quickly during this activity. Encourage the children to explore several ideas by moving shapes around until they have their best idea. Then they should get the glue. If glue is provided at the beginning of the activity, some children glue the shapes down with less thought.

Completing the Activity:

1. Provide each student with the appropriate Shapes handout.

2. Say:

   "Cut out each shape on this paper (hold up handout) so you can use the shapes to solve a problem. After they are cut out, look at them and think about them. Move them around and think about how they could go together to...
   (Read only the one problem below which is appropriate to the students' grade level.)

Grade	Problem
Second	*"...make something found at school that helps people in some way."*
Third	*"...make something found at home that helps people in some way."*
Fourth	*"...make something found in a store that helps people in some way."*
Fifth	*"...make something found outside that helps people in some way."*
Sixth	*"...make something found in a hole that helps people in some way."*

   "You must use all the shapes and you may not cut them to make them smaller."

   *"There are lots of different ways to use the shapes to solve the problem. Keep thinking until you have a really good idea. When you have thought of your **best** idea, get some glue and glue the shapes on your paper the way you want them to go together. Then, write a few words or sentences to explain what you've made and how it helps others."*

3. Occasionally, a student will want to use a pencil or crayons to add details. It is appropriate for students to do so after they have glued the shapes to show their best idea.

4. Depending on their level of development, some students are only able to attend to one attribute of the problems. For example, when asked to "... make something found at school that helps people in some way," some second graders created something found at school but they could not also explain how it helped people.

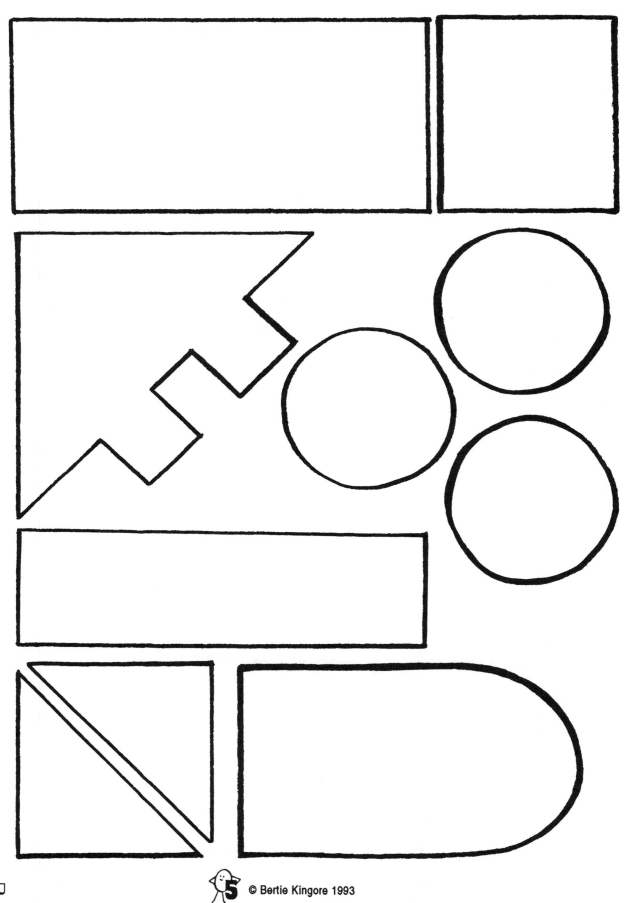

REBUS STORIES

Evaluation guidelines are on page 102

Date due: _____   Teacher: _____

School: _____

Objective:

Student will have an opportunity to demonstrate meaning motivation, sense of humor, analytical thinking and advanced language by creating a rebus story.

Materials:

Introduction pictures and masking tape, or overhead transparency of introduction pictures.

Handout of rebus pictures appropriate to grade level. The pictures are repeated on each page. Therefore, kindergarteners need only 1/4 page; grades 1-6 need 1/2 page. Extra copies of the pictures should be available for any child who wants to use multiple copies of the pictures in a story.

Scissors

Glue

Pencils

Preparing for the Activity:

1. This activity is untimed and may be administered in whole group, small groups or individual settings. Most students will complete the activity in approximately 20 minutes. Some will take longer to complete the writing of their story.

2. Encourage individuality (see Suggestions for Encouraging Individuality on page 67) or arrange student's working space out of the view of others.

3. To demonstrate the activity on the chalkboard, cut apart the Introduction pictures and use loops of masking tape on each so it will adhere to the chalkboard. To demonstrate the activity on the overhead, make a transparency of the Introduction pictures and cut them apart.

4. Do not provide glue too soon. Encourage the children to manipulate the pictures and think of their best idea before they begin to glue the pictures in place.

Demonstrating the Activity:

1. Display the Introduction pictures.

"These pictures can be put together in any order to create a story. For example, if I arrange them like this (character without glasses, character with glasses, crayon and cat) *I can tell a story."*

Write the words on the chalkboard or overhead as you tell the story and put each picture in its appropriate place.

"This kid (character without glasses) *and the dad* (character with glasses) went to the store to buy some new crayons (pictures) *for school. They were surprised to find that the store was run by a cat* (picture)*! The cat said they had to draw a picture of her before they could buy the crayons. So they colored a funny picture of her. The cat liked it so much that she went home to live with them."*

"Now let's mix them up and make a new story. Let's put the cat picture first. Think a minute. Who could this be? (Show character without glasses.) *What happens next? Tell me which pictures to put next and tell me what words to use to tell what happens with each picture."*

2. Continue until all the pictures have been used in the story. Model writing the words to accompany the story the children have dictated.

Completing the Activity:

1. After the students are familiar with the idea of making rebus stories, show them the handout of rebus pictures.

2. Say to the students:

"Here are some different pictures. Cut them apart by cutting on the lines of these boxes around the pictures."

If you are not sure your children understand, cut as you talk to demonstrate what you mean. It is not "wrong" if the children cut around each picture but the intention is to simplify the cutting task and concentrate time for thinking and meaning development.

"Think about your pictures after you cut them out. Move them around. Mix them up. Think about a story that no one else might think of. Think about lots of funny things or different things that might happen in this story. When you have thought of your best idea, write your story and glue each picture where it belongs. Remember to use all of the pictures in your story. Write your name on the back of your story."

3. You may provide extra copies of the pictures if children ask for them. The task requires students to use all of the pictures at least once and figure out how to combine them to reach a meaningful story. It is certainly appropriate if children want to use multiple copies of the picture so they have a picture to glue in place each time that picture reoccurs in their story.

4. To simplify the process, kindergarten and/or first grade teachers may have students simply glue their pictures in sequence in one row and then write the story underneath. You may also need to or prefer to take dictation from each student and write each story after the children have glued the pictures in place (see Suggestions for Taking Dictation on pages 68-70).

Ask each student *individually* to tell you his/her story.
Say to each student:

"Tell me your story about these pictures."

If more explanation is desired, say:

"Tell me some more about your story."

To insure equality and fairness to all students, limit prompting about the pictures to the two statements above.

REBUS STORIES

Introduction Pictures

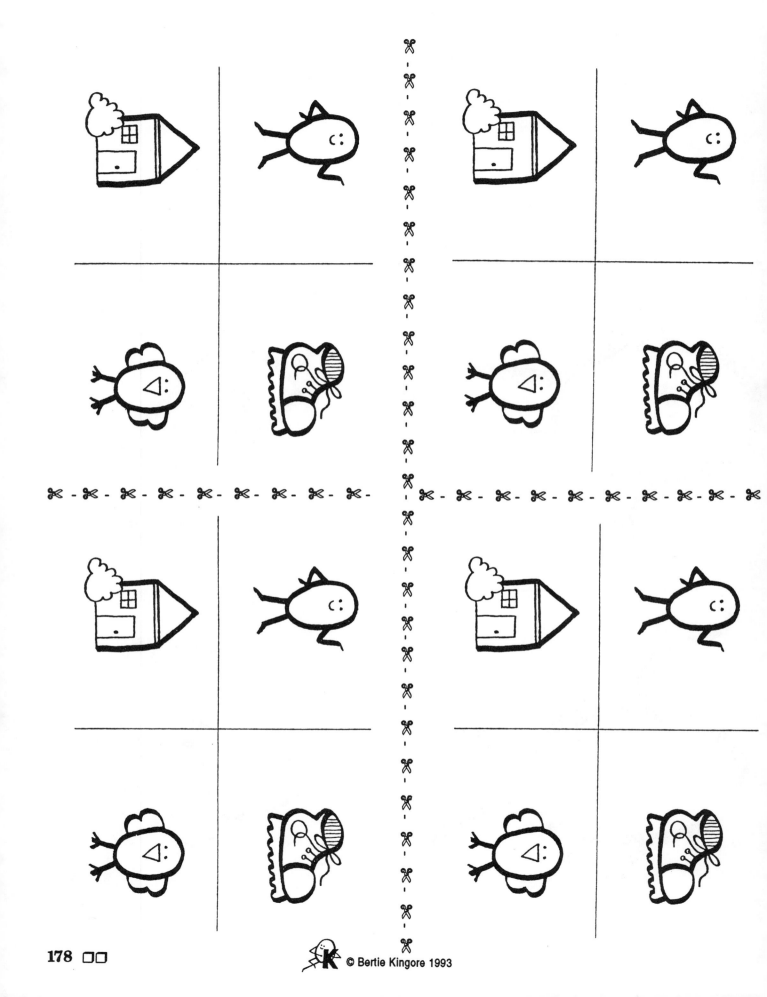

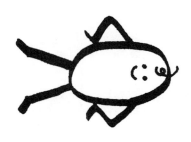

✂ - ✂ - ✂ - ✂ - ✂ - ✂ - ✂ - ✂ - ✂ - ✂ - ✂ - ✂ - ✂ - ✂ - ✂ - ✂ - ✂ -

□□ **179**

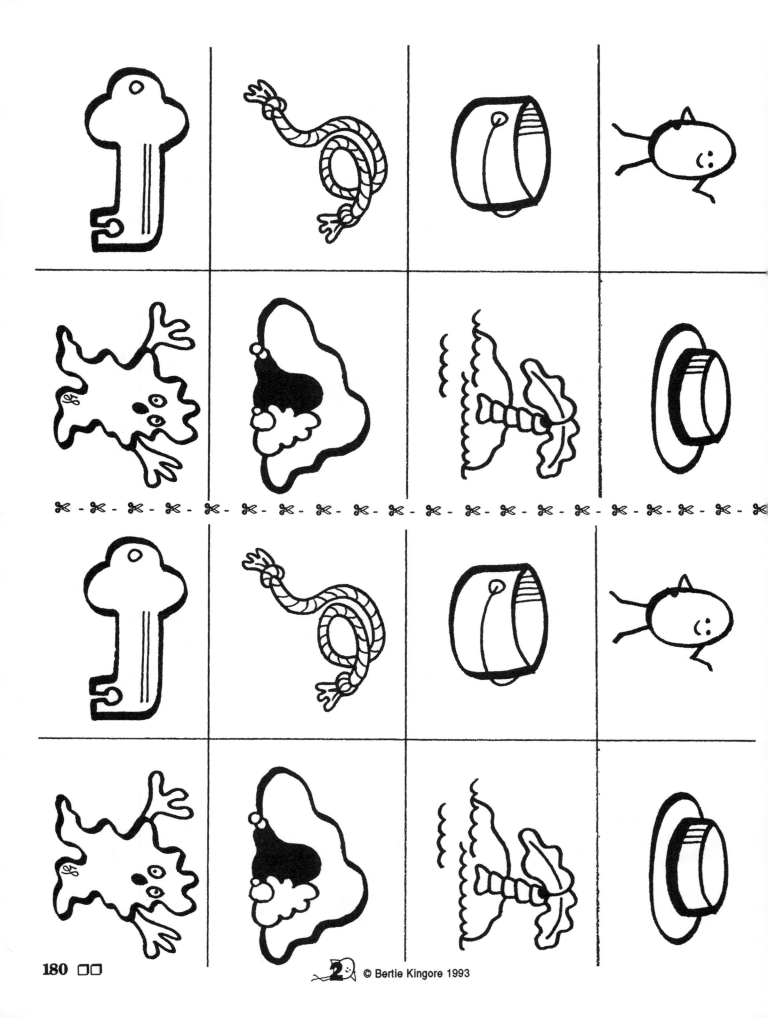

□□

181

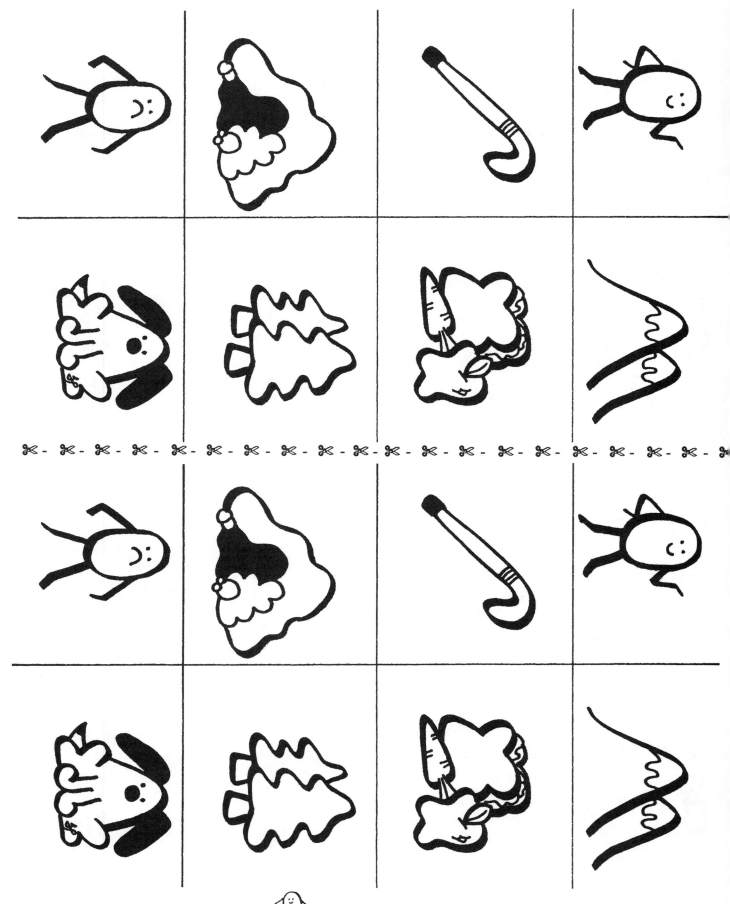

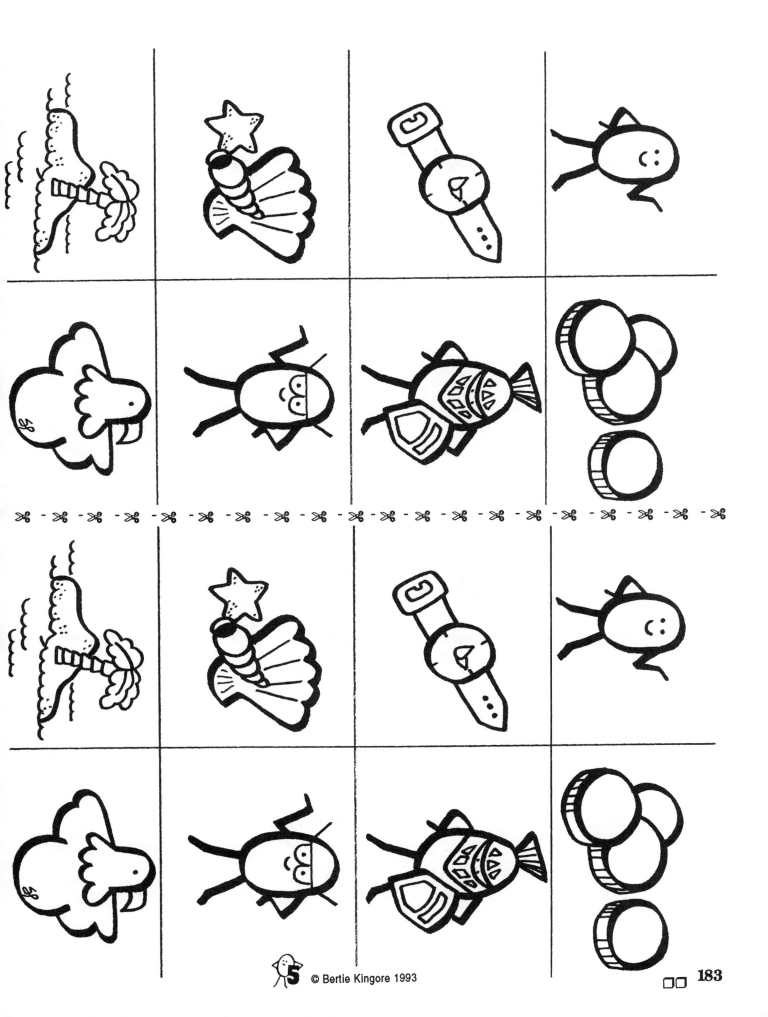

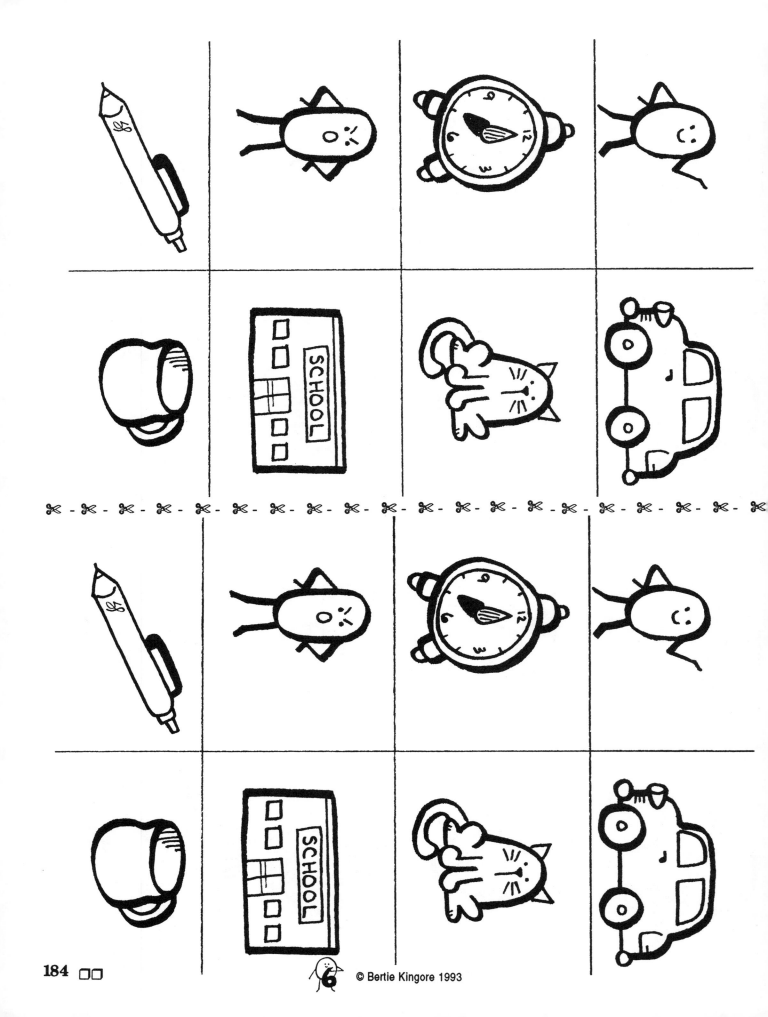

Planned Experiences

Using

Children's Literature
Copies of Activities

Notes & Comments

Animals Should Definitely Not Wear Clothing.
Evaluation Guidelines on Page 103

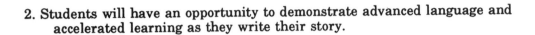

Objectives:

1. Students will have an opportunity to demonstrate analytical thinking and sense of humor by creating pictures and ideas for a new story using the sentence pattern from the book <u>Animals Should Definitely Not Wear Clothing.</u>

2. Students will have an opportunity to demonstrate advanced language and accelerated learning as they write their story.

Materials:

Book - <u>Animals Should Definitely Not Wear Clothing</u>.
by Judi Barrett (Atheneum, 1970).

Story pattern page

Pencils, crayons or markers

Optional: glue and construction paper scraps.

Preparing for the Activity

1. Read the title of the book aloud to the children. Tell the children that the author, Judi Barrett, thinks there would be plenty of trouble if animals wore clothing. Ask the children to look at the cover and predict some of the troubles that animals might have if they wore clothing.

2. Expressively read the book to the children without elaborating on the concepts.

Demonstrating the Activity

1. Say to the children:

"We can make up a new story like this one. Let's think of something people do all the time that would be really funny if animals did it. For example, let's say that animals should definitely <u>not</u> drive a car. Brainstorm with me all the funny things that might happen if animals drove a car."

2. Write down the children's responses. Encourage lots of different ideas.

"Try to think of something else no one has thought of."

3. Say:

"Let's choose some of your ideas to write a story. Animals should definitely
      <u>not</u> drive a car because _____ (repeat one of their ideas)   ,
      because ____(repeat another idea), and most of all, because
      _____ (repeat another idea) _____.

Completing the Activity

1. Provide each child with a copy of the story pattern.

   "Now I want each of you to make up your own story. Think of
   something else that people do which would be funny if animals
   did it. Try to think of something no one else will think of. Then
   brainstorm lots of funny things that might happen. When you
   have thought of your best ideas, write your story on this paper
   and use crayons or markers to make a picture.

2. If desired, children may also use construction paper scraps and glue to
   complete their pictures. It is best if all involved classrooms jointly
   agree whether or not to use this option.

3. This activity is untimed. Teachers may explain all of the directions and
   allow the children to work independently as long as they need. Thus,
   this activity works well during that part of the day when children are
   scheduled to complete independent seat work. Most children will
   complete their pictures and stories in about twenty-five minutes.

4. If desired, the stories may be put together to make a class book for
   the children to read and enjoy. The title might be: **"Animals**
   Should Definitely Not."

Animals should definitely <u>not</u> _____

_____

_____

_____

_____

because _____ ,

_____

_____

_____

because _____ ,

_____

_____

_____

and most of all, because _____ ,

_____

_____

_____

_____ .

Donna O'Neeshuck Was Chased by Some Cows
Evaluation Guidelines on Page 104

Objectives:

1. Students will have an opportunity to demonstrate analytical thinking, meaning motivation, sense of humor and sensitivity to creating a new story.

2. Students will have an opportunity to demonstrate advanced language as they write their stories.

Materials:

Book: <u>DONNA O'NEESHUCK WAS CHASED BY SOME COWS</u> by Bill Grossman (Harper Trophy, 1988)

Paper

Pencil or pen; crayons or markers

Preparing for the Activity

1. Read the title of the book to the students and show them the cover. Brainstorm why cows might be chasing Donna O'Neeshuck.

2. Expressively read the book to the students without elaborating on the concepts.

Completing the Activity

1. Say to the students:

"Now each of you can write a story. Think of something about you that would make people want to follow you. It might be something funny or something more serious, but think about a quality you have or something you do that might make others follow you. You may choose to write your story in rhyme as Bill Grossman did, but your story does not have to rhyme. When your story is finished, draw one or more pictures to illustrate your story."

2. This activity is untimed. Teachers may explain all of the directions and allow the students to work independently as long as they need. Thus, this activity works well during that part of the day when students are scheduled to complete independent seat work. Most students will complete their pictures and stories in about thirty minutes to one hour.

3. A few students may need more help to prompt an idea for their story. One or more of the following ideas might be shared one-to-one with a student having trouble beginning his/her story.

What is something people notice about you?

What is something you do well?

What do you collect?

What is something you really care about?

What is something you might do that might make others laugh or want to watch you?

What is something you have that others might want to see?

4. If desired, the stories and illustrations may be posted on a bulletin board or put together in a class book so the students may read and enjoy each other's creations. Much discussion among students will result.

A House is a House for Me.
Evaluation Guidelines on Page 105

Objectives:

1. Students will have an opportunity to demonstrate perspective, sense of humor and analytical thinking by creating additional examples of things that are houses.

2. Students will have an opportunity to demonstrate advanced language and accelerated learning as they write sentences to tell about their ideas and illustrations.

Materials:

Book - <u>A House is a House for Me</u> by Mary Ann Hoberman (Puffin Books, 1982)

Overhead transparency of sentence pattern - optional

Paper

Pencils, crayons or markers

Preparing for the Activity

The book is somewhat long and includes so many examples that it limits students' ability to think of additional ideas. Therefore, the activity works best if you plan to read about one-third of the book to the students before having them complete the activity. Begin at the beginning of the book and read far enough that you believe students understand the concept. Then skip to the last pages and read them for closure. Read expressively without stopping to discuss the examples.

Demonstrating the Activity

1. Say to the students:

   "We can think of some different things that are houses."

Use an overhead transparency of the sentence pattern on page 194 or write the sentence pattern on the chalkboard.

   "Brainstorm with me some new examples of things that are houses and I'll write your ideas in this sentence pattern like the one in Mary Ann Hoberman's book."

2. Write down several of the students' responses. Encourage lots of different ideas.

   "Try to think of something no one else has thought of."

Completing the Activity

1. Provide each student with paper, pencil and markers or crayons.

   *"Now each of you can write your own ideas. Think of things that were not shown in the book. Think of different things that could be houses. Some of your ideas may be serious and some may be funny. Use the sentence pattern and write **several** ideas. You may write your ideas in rhyme as the book did if you want to, but try to write ideas no one else will think of. Draw a picture to illustrate each of your ideas."*

2. This activity is untimed. Teachers may explain all of the directions and allow the students to work independently as long as they need. Thus, this activity works well during that part of the way when students are scheduled to complete independent seat work. Most students will complete their pictures and ideas in twenty to thirty minutes.

3. When all the students have completed the activity, allow opportunities for students to share their ideas and pictures with others in the class. Then, read the rest of the book and ask students to note which ideas they had that are/are not in the book.

4. If desired, the pages may be put together to make a class book for the students to read and enjoy.

A _____ is a house

for _____.

A _____ is a house

for _____.

A _____ is a house

for _____.

A _____ is a house

for _____.

A _____ is a house

for _____.

I'm Coming to Get You!
Evaluation Guidelines on Page 106

Objectives:

1. Students will have an opportunity to demonstrate perspective, analytical thinking and sense of humor by creating a new episode for the book I'M COMING TO GET YOU!

2. Students will have an opportunity to demonstrate advanced language as they write or dictate words to tell about their pictures.

Materials:

Book - I'm Coming to Get You ! by Tony Ross (Dial Books, 1984).

Paper

Pencils, crayons or markers

Preparing for the Activity:

1. Tell the children that the author, Tony Ross, wrote this book for his little three-year-old daughter. She was afraid of monsters and he wanted to show her that imaginary monsters may seem scary at first, but really they are nothing at all.

2. Expressively read the book to the children without stopping to discuss the events or concepts.

Completing the Activity:

1. Say to the children:

"We can make up a new part for this story. Let's pretend that Tommy went on to school. In his class, the kids were doing things and working just like we are. His classroom even looked a lot like ours.

"Let's pretend that the monster follows Tommy to his school. Draw a picture of Tommy doing something at school and show the monster trying to get him again. Think of a really good idea that is not like anyone elses. Write your story at the bottom of your picture."

2. This activity is untimed. Teachers may explain all of the directions and allow the children to work independently as long as they need. Thus, this activity works well during that part of the day when children are scheduled to complete independent seat work. Most children will complete their pictures and stories in about thirty minutes.

3. If the child's writing is unclear or undeveloped, say: *"Tell me some more about your picture."* Write the child's explanation on the back of the picture, using as many of the child's words as possible. (See Suggestions for Taking Dictation on pages 68-70).

It Looked Like Spilt Milk
Evaluation Guidelines on page 107

Date due: _____

Teacher: _____

School: _____

Objectives:

1. Students will have an opportunity to demonstrate perspective, analytical thinking and sense of humor by creating pictures and ideas <u>IT LOOKED LIKE SPILT MILK</u>.

2. Students will have an opportunity to demonstrate advanced language as they write or dictate words to tell about their pictures.

Materials:

Book - <u>It Looked Like Spilt Milk</u> by Charles G. Shaw (Scholastic, 1947).

Duplicated sentence pattern; cut apart so it makes five separate sentence strips.

Blue construction paper; fold down the top third of the paper.

White tempera paint.

Plastic teaspoon

Pencils

Glue

Demonstrating the Activity:

1. Read the book to the children in an expressive manner but without discussing concepts.

2. Talk with the children about the shapes of clouds. Ask children to talk about any shapes they may have seen in the clouds or any shapes they think they might be able to see in the clouds. (If there are visible clouds, you may wish to go outside to look at their shapes and talk about what the shapes could be.)

3. Demonstrate shapes by spooning one or more blobs of white paint in the fold of one piece of the construction paper. Fold the paper down over the blob. Gently rub your hand over the paper to spread the paint inside. Open the fold to discover with the children what shape you have made. The picture will use the top two-thirds of the paper, thus leaving the bottom third of the page for the sentence strip.

4. Talk together about what real things or funny things this cloud shape could be. Turn the paper around and upside down. Encourage children to try to see many different ideas in each different position. Encourage the children to brainstorm as many real things and as many funny ideas as they can.

5. Choose their favorite idea for what the shape could be, write it on one of the duplicated sentence pattern strips and glue that strip at the bottom of the page. Encourage the students to use more than one word to complete the idea, such as "a crazy upside-down dragon" instead of just a "a dragon". Tell the children that this picture could be used as a new event in a story about spilt milk.

Completing the Activity:

1. Let each child use the paint and construction paper to make his/her own cloud shape. Each then writes or dictates his/her idea for the sentence pattern and glues the sentence strip at the bottom of the construction paper .(See Suggestions for Taking Dictation on pages 68-70.)

2. If desired, the pictures may be put together to make a class book for the children to read and enjoy.

Sometimes it looked like

But it wasn't.

_____

Sometimes it looked like

But it wasn't.

_____

Sometimes it looked like

But it wasn't.

_____

Sometimes it looked like

But it wasn't.

_____

Sometimes it looked like

But it wasn't.

_____

The Paper Bag Princess
Evaluation Guidelines on Page 108

Date: _____   Teacher: _____

School: _____

Objectives:

Students will have an opportunity to demonstrate advanced language, analytical thinking, sense of humor and sensitivity by creating a modern folk tale.

Materials:

Book - The Paper Bag Princess by Robert Munsch (Annick Press Ltd., 1980).

Venn diagram overhead transparency - optional

Pencil or pen; crayons or markers

Paper

Preparing for the Activity

1. Read the title of the book and explain that this is not a traditional folk tale. The author, Robert Munsch, is using the style of a folk tale to tell a story with more contemporary values and characters.

2. Expressively read the book to the students.

Demonstrating the Activity

Use the overhead transparency of a Venn diagram or draw one on the chalkboard. Discuss with the students ways in which the book both differs from and is similar to traditional folk tales. Record the students' ideas in the appropriate areas of the diagram.

Completing the Activity

1. Say to the students"
"Now each of you can write a story in the style of a folk tale. Think about current situations or contemporary events. Create one or more characters who have today's values and needs. Place that character or characters in a folk tale setting and write what happens. Your story might be funny or serious. When your story is finished, draw one or more pictures to illustrate your story."

2. This activity is untimed. Teachers may explain all of the directions and allow the students to work independently as long as they need. Thus, this activity works well during that part of the day when students are scheduled to complete independent seat work. Most students will complete their pictures and stories in forty-five minutes to one hour.

3. If possible, the stories and illustrations should be placed on a bulletin board or put together in a class book so the students may read and enjoy each other's creations. Ongoing comparison and contrast will naturally occur as students read and discuss these stories.

200

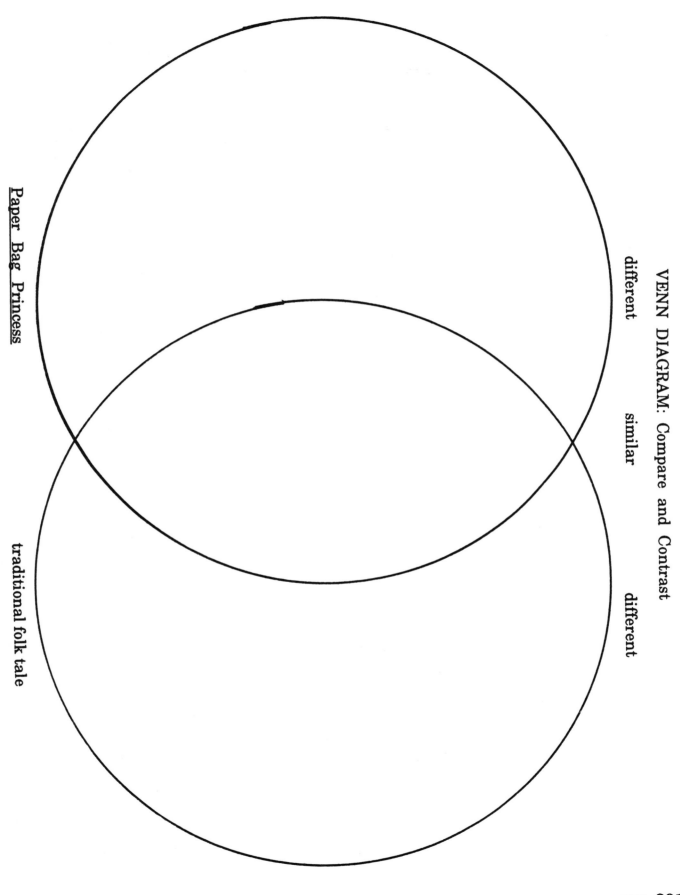

VENN DIAGRAM: Compare and Contrast

different

similar

different

Paper Bag Princess

traditional folk tale

Q is for Duck
Evaluation Guidelines on page 109

Date Due: _____   Teacher _____

School _____

Objectives:

1. Students will have an opportunity to demonstrate analytical thinking, meaning motivation and sense of humor by creating pictures and ideas for a new story using the sentence pattern from the book <u>Q is for Duck</u>.

2. Students will have an opportunity to demonstrate advanced language as they write or dictate words to tell their own pictures.

Materials:

Book: <u>Q is for Duck</u> by Mary Elting and Michael Folsom. (Clarion Books, 1980).

Sentence pattern page 204

Pencils, crayons or markers.

Preparing for the Activity:

1. This activity is untimed and may be administered in whole class, small groups or individual settings. Most students will complete this activity in approximately fifteen minutes.

2. Show the cover of the book to the children. Explain that the authors want this to be a guessing game by having us guess what we think the next page might be.

3. Expressively read the book to the children. After reading a couple of pages as examples, begin asking the children to predict each letter's connection before you turn the page. Be aware of the children who demonstrate analytical reasoning through an occasional unusual but appropriate response. Also note the children who laugh to show understanding of the pages with more subtle humor, e.g., the "because" pages for letters B, D, F.

Demonstrating the Activity:

1. Say to the children:

> *"We are going to make our own book like Q is for Duck.*
> *But our book will be about children instead of animals.*
> *The title of our book is X is for Our Class. I will finish*
> *the X page by using one of these pages."* (Show the sentence
> pattern page and read it with the children.)

2. As the children watch, write:

"X is for our class.

"Why?

"Because children in our class are excellent and exciting thinkers."

Completing the Activity:

1. Hand out the duplicated sentence pattern page and ask children to write
   their name on the back.

> *"Now I want each of you to make up your own page for*
> *our book. First, decide on which letter of the alphabet*
> *you want to use. Then think of something about*
> *children which is serious or funny and begins with*
> *that letter. Try to think of things no one else will think*
> *of. Then you can write your best idea on this paper*
> *and draw a picture to go with your idea."*

2. Responses will be more individual if children using the same
   letter do not sit near each other.

3. The teacher is encouraged to take dictation for any child for whom
   writing is too difficult. The teacher may also record responses on
   the back of any page for which clarification is needed. (See
   Suggestions for Taking Dictation on pages 68-70.)

4. As much as is possible, note on the back of the finished pages which
   children especially demonstrated analytical thinking or sense of
   humor when you first read Q is for Duck to the class.

5. Note on the back of the finished pages which children could not finish
   the pattern without adult help.

_____ is for our class.

Why?

Because children _____

_____

_____.

Your picture.

The Surprise
Evaluation Guidelines on Page 110

Date due: _____   Teacher: _____

School: _____

Objectives:

1. Students will have the opportunity to use analytical thinking, meaning motivation and sensitivity to plan a surprise for someone else.

2. Students will have the opportunity to use advanced language to write or tell about their plan.

Materials:

Book - <u>The Surprise</u> by George Shannon (Greenwillow Books, 1983).

Paper

Pencils, crayons or markers

Preparing for the Activity

1. This activity is untimed and may be administered in whole class, small groups, or individual settings. Most students will complete this activity in ten to fifteen minutes.

2. Encourage individual responses or arrange for individual work spaces. (See suggestions for Encouraging Individuality on page 67.)

3. Talk with the children about what a surprise is and what kinds of surprises any of them might have had.

4. Expressively read the book to the children without stopping to discuss details.

Completing the Activity

1. Say to the children:

   "The character in the story really used his head. He planned a good surprise to help someone feel happy."

   *"Now I want to plan a **good** surprise. What is something that you could really do for someone else that would be very good for that person and make that person feel very happy? Think of someone you would like to make happy. What could you do for a happy surprise? Draw a picture of your idea. Think of a good idea that is not like anyone elses. Think of something you could really do to help someone."*

2. Give each child a piece of paper. Ask them to write their names on the back of the paper.

   "Draw a picture showing your idea on this paper."

3. As each child finishes his/her picture, say:

   "Tell me about your surprise. How did it make someone happy?"
   Write the child's explanation on the back of the picture using as many of the child's words as possible. (See Suggestions for Taking Dictation on pages 68-70.) If the child's ideas are unclear or unelaborative, say:

   "Tell me some more to help me understand what you mean."

Ten Black Dots
Evaluation Guidelines on page 111

Date due:_____   Teacher: _____

School: _____

Objectives:

1. The students will have the opportunity to use analytical thinking, meaning motivation and perspective to complete a picture using ten black dots.

2. Students will have the opportunity to use advanced language to write or tell about their picture.

Materials:

Book - <u>Ten Black Dots</u> by Donald Drews (Greenwillow Books, 1986)

Sentence strips from handout

Black stick-on dots, one-half to one inch size; one set of ten dots for each child.
(If preferred, black construction paper dots and glue may be substituted for stick-on dots.).

Paper

Pencils, crayons or markers

Preparing for the Activity:

1. This activity is untimed and may be administered in whole class, small groups, or individual settings. Most students will complete this activity in approximately fifteen minutes.

2. Encourage individual responses or arrange for individual work spaces. (See Suggestions for Encouraging Individuality on page 67.)

3. Some children will put the dots together to make something. Others will make a picture around the dots. Either process is appropriate as long as they figure out how to use all ten dots in their picture.

Demonstrating the Activity:

1. Read the book to the children in an expressive manner but without discussing details.

2. Stop reading after finishing the page that tells about the **nine** black dots.

3. Say to the children:
"We get to make up the next part of this story. I have ten black dots for each of you. You can move them around on your paper until you think of a good idea for something you can do with the ten black dots. Try to think of an idea that no one else may think of. Plan carefully and think about what you can make. When you think of your best idea, peel off the back of each dot (if you are using stick-on dots) *and stick each one where you need it on your paper."*

(Demonstrate moving the dots around on a piece of paper before peeling off the backing. Then demonstrate how to peel off the backing on a dot.)

"After you stick your dots on your paper you can use your crayons (or markers) and pencil to draw the rest of your picture. Then glue one of these sentence strips on the bottom of your paper and write about your picture. I will help you write your sentence if you need me to."

(Show the children one of the sentence strips cuts from the handout.)

Completing the Activity

1. Give each child ten black dots, a sentence strip and paper. Ask them to write their names on the back of their paper. Encourage them again to plan what they can make before they peel the backing off of the dots.

2. As each child finishes his/her picture, remind each to complete the sentence strip. Take dictation from the children for whom you deem it necessary.

10   Ten dots can make

✂ - ✂ - ✂ - ✂ - ✂ - ✂ - ✂ - ✂ - ✂ - ✂ - ✂ - ✂ - ✂ - ✂ - ✂ - ✂

10   Ten dots can make

✂ - ✂ - ✂ - ✂ - ✂ - ✂ - ✂ - ✂ - ✂ - ✂ - ✂ - ✂ - ✂ - ✂ - ✂ - ✂

10   Ten dots can make

✂ - ✂ - ✂ - ✂ - ✂ - ✂ - ✂ - ✂ - ✂ - ✂ - ✂ - ✂ - ✂ - ✂ - ✂ - ✂

10   Ten dots can make

Two Bad Ants
Evaluation Guidelines on Page 112

Objectives:

Students will have an opportunity to demonstrate advanced language, analytical thinking, perspective, sense of humor and sensitivity by creating a sequel for the story.

Materials:

Book - <u>Two Bad Ants</u> by Chris Van Allsburg (Houghton Mifflin, 1988).

Paper

Pencil or pen; crayons or markers

Preparing for the Activity

Expressively read the book to the students without elaborating on the concepts.

Completing the Activity

1. Say:

"I want each of you to write a sequel to this story. In this sequel, two scout ants find a new and wonderful discovery at a school. The building and surrounding area look a lot like ours; students are doing things and working just as we are. Think how school things might look to ants and what they might call each thing they encounter. For example, a brick wall in the The Two Bad Ants was called a mountain."

To clarify this point, you may wish to hold up page 10 of the book and show students the picture of the wall.

"Think of some really good ideas that are not like everyone elses. Plan what the two bad ants do on this visit to a school. What do they investigate and what happens to them because of their size and curiosity? Include in your story how the ants feel as things happen. Write your story and draw one or several pictures to illustrate how things look to the ants."

2. This activity is untimed. Teachers may explain all of the directions and allow the students to work independently as long as they need. Thus, this activity works well during that part of the day when students are scheduled to complete independent seat work. Most students will complete their pictures and stories in thirty minutes to one hour.

What Can You Do With a Pocket?
Evaluation Guidelines on page 113

Date due: _____   Teacher: _____

School: _____

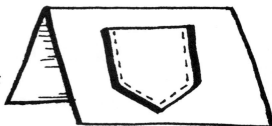

Objectives:

1. Students will have opportunity to use analytical thinking, sense of humor, and accelerated learning through clues and sentence completion.

2. Students will have opportunity to express meaning motivation and advanced language through their illustrations and explanations.

Materials:

Optional: Book <u>What Can You Do with a Pocket?</u> by Eve Merriam (DLM,1990)

Picture cards to fit in a pocket.

9 x 12 paper folded in half

Pencils, crayons or markers

Glue or paste

Magazine pages

Clothing item with a pocket

Preparing for the Activity:

1. This activity is untimed and is best introduced in whole class or small group settings. Most students will complete this activity in twenty minutes.

2. Encourage individual responses or arrange for individual work spaces. (See Suggestions for Encouraging Individuality on page 67.)

Demonstrating the Activity:

1. Optional: Expressively read to the children, <u>What Can You Do with a Pocket</u>? Discuss how the author used her imagination to think of things people could put in their pockets and what imaginative and funny things people could do with those things.

2. Provide an item of clothing that has a pocket. Place picture cards in the pocket and allow students to pick a card and complete the sentence

"In this pocket there is a _____."

3. Mix up the cards. This time, before showing a card, say one or two clues about the picture, e.g. *"It is a pet. It wags its tail when it sees me."*

   Let the children guess what the picture shows. (dog)

4. Move from the concrete to abstract by asking for volunteers to think of something else that could be in a pocket. As a group, name two or three clues that could be used to tell about that item or to tell about what you could do with that item.

Completing the Activity:

1. Provide paper for the children to fold in half. Working individually, have students draw a pocket on the outside. They then open the paper and draw or cut out from a magazine a picture of something to glue on the inside of their paper.

2. Establish a game-like atmosphere and encourage the children to keep their ideas a secret so everyone may guess later.

3. Have each child think of three clues as to what is **in** the pocket or three clues as to what could be **done** with the thing in the pocket. Remind them that they **might** think of funny or imaginative things. Say to the children:
   "When you have thought of your three best clues, write them on the back of your folded paper. You can read them aloud later and let everyone guess what is in your pocket or what you could do with it. Write your name on the back of your paper."

4. Later, let each child show his/her pocket and read the clues while the others guess.

What's Claude Doing?
Evaluation Guidelines on page 114.

Date due: _____   Teacher _____

School _____

Objective:

The students will have an opportunity to demonstrate advanced language, analytical thinking, meaning motivation, and sensitivity by writing about helping others.

Materials:

Book: <u>What's Claude Doing?</u> by Dick Gackenbach (Clarion Books, 1984)

Paper, lined or unlined as preferred

Pencil, crayons or markers

Preparing for the Activity:

1. This activity is untimed. The teacher may explain all of the directions and allow the children to work independently as long as they need. Thus, this activity works well during that part of the day when children are scheduled to complete independent seat work. Most children will complete their pictures and stories in about twenty minutes.

2. Expressively read the book to the class without pausing to discuss the events.

3. Stop after reading the page toward the end of the book which has the text: "'What's Claude Doing?' all the animals wondered." Ask the children to predict what Claude is doing. Note which children express especially insightful responses. Then finish reading the book.

4. Talk with the children about how Claude helped someone even though it meant he missed other fun things.

Completing the Activity:

1. Say to the children:

"*We are going to work together to write a book about helping others. Sometimes people or animals need help. There are things kids can't really do, of course. But there are also lots of things you **could** do to help. Think of things you really can do to help others. Write your best ideas on this paper. Tell who you will help and how you will help. Then draw a picture to show how you are helping.*"

2. Write on the chalkboard the following sentence pattern for the children to copy on their paper.

I can help _____

by _____

_____

_____

_____.

3. Ask children to write their names on the back of their paper.

4. The teacher is encouraged to take dictation for any child for whom writing is too difficult. The teacher may also record responses on the back of any page for which clarification is needed. (See Suggestions for Taking Dictation on pages 68-70.)

5. If desired, the stories may be put together to make a class book for the children to read and enjoy. The title might be: WE CAN HELP!

Teacher Resources:
Children's Literature

Barrett, Judi. (1970). <u>Animals Should Definitely Not Wear Clothing</u>. Bloomfield, Conn.: Atheneum.

Crews, Donald. (1986). <u>Ten Black Dots.</u> New York: Greenwillow Books.

Elting, Mary and Michael Folsom. (1980). <u>Q is for Duck</u>. New York: Clarion Books.

Gackenbach, Dick. (1984). <u>What's Claude Doing?</u> New York: Clarion Books.

Grossman, Bill. (1988). <u>Donna O'Neeschuck Was Chased by Some Cows</u>. New York: Harper Trophy.

Hoberman, Mary Ann. (1982). <u>A House Is a House for Me</u>. New York: Puffin Books.

Merriam, Eve. (1990). <u>What Can You Do with a Pocket?</u> Ellen, Texas: DLM.

Munsch, Robert N. (1980). <u>Paper Bag Princess</u>. Toronto, Canada: Annick Press Ltd.

Ross, Tony. (1984). <u>I'm Coming To Get You</u>. New York: Dial Books.

Shannon, George. (1983). <u>The Surprise</u>. New York: Greenwillow Books.

Shaw, Charles G. (1947. <u>It Looked Like Spilt Milk</u>. New York: Scholastic.

Silverstein, Shel. (1974). <u>Where the Sidewalks Ends</u>. New York: Harper & Row.

Van Allsburg, Chris. (1988). <u>Two Bad Ants</u>. Boston: Houghlin Mifflin Co.

References

Alvino, J. & Wieler, J. (1979). How standardized testing fails to identify the gifted and what teachers can do about it. Phi Delta Kappan, 61(2), 106-109.

Bernal, E.M., Jr. (1978). The identification of gifted Chicano children. In A.Y. Baldwin, G.H. Gear, & L.J. Lucito (Eds.), Educational planning for the gifted: Overcoming cultural, geographic and socioeconomic barriers (pp. 14-17). Reston, VA: The Council for Exceptional Children.

Brandt, R. (1988). On assessment in the arts: A conversation with Howard Gardner. Educational Leadership, 45(4), 30-34.

California Mathematics Council (1989). Assessment Alternatives in Mathematics, Berkeley, CA: EQUALS, Lawrence Hall of Science.

Chapman, C. (1990). Authentic Writing Assessment. (Washington, DC: ERIC Digest No. EDO TM 90 4).

Costa, A.L. (1989). Re-assessing assessment. Educational Leadership, 46(7), 1.

Flood, J. & Lapp D. (1989). Reporting reading progress: A comparison portfolio for parents. The Reading Teacher, 41(3), 508-514.

Ford, D.Y. & Harris, J.J., III (1990). On discovering the hidden treasure of gifted and talented Black children. Roeper Review, 13(1), 27-32.

Gardner, Howard & Hatch, Thomas (1989). Multiple intelligences go to school. Educational Researcher, 18(8), 4-10.

Hagen, E. (1980). Identification of the gifted. New York: Teachers College Press.

Hiebert, E.H. & Calfee, R.C. (1989). Advancing academic literacy through teacher assessments. Educational Leadership, 46(7), 50-54.

Karnes, M.B. (1987). Issues in educating young gifted children: Promising practices. Indianapolis: Indiana Department of Education. (ERIC Document Reproduction Service No. ED 315 946).

Kingore, B.W. (1990). The Kingore observation inventory. Des Moines: Leadership Publishers.

Kirst, M.W. (1991). Educational Researcher. (Washington, DC: American Educational Research Association).

Kitano, M.K. & Kirby, D.F. (1986). Gifted education: A comprehensive view. Boston: Little, Brown & Co.

Long, J. & Clemmons, M. (1982). Creating classroom situations to encourage the display of gifted behaviors: An aide to identification. Gifted Child Today. 35, 38-40.

Maeroff, G.I. (1991). Assessing Alternative Assessment. Phi Delta Kappan, 73(12), 273-281.

Marland, S.P., Jr. (1971). Education of the gifted and talented (Vols. 1 & 2). Washington, D.C.: U.S. Department of Health, Education, and Welfare.

Mills, R.P. (1989). Portfolios capture rich array of student performance. The School Administrator, 46(11), 8-11.

Paulson, F.L., Paulson, P.R. & Meyer, C.A. (1991) What makes a Portfolio a Portfolio? Educational Leadership , 48(2), 60-64.

Paulson, F.L. & Paulson, P.R. (1990, August). How Do Portfolios Measure Up? Paper presented at the Northwest Evaluation Association, Union, WA.

Ramsey, K. (1990, October 19). Writing tests help teachers evaluate student performance. Burlington Free Press.

Richert, E.S. (1987). Rampant problems and promising practices in the identification of disadvantaged gifted students. Gifted Child Quarterly, 31(4), 149-154.

Richert, E.S., Alvino, J.J., & McDonnel, R.C. (1982). National report on identification: Assessment and recommendations for comprehensive identification of gifted and talented youth. Sewell, NJ: Educational Improvement Center-South.

Rimm, S. (1984). The characteristics approach: Identification and beyond. Gifted Child Quarterly, 28(4), 181-187.

Roedell, W.C., Jackson, N.E., & Robinson, H.B. (1980). Gifted young children. New York: Teachers College Press.

Rothman, R. (1990). Large 'faculty meeting' ushers in pioneering assessment in Vermont. Education Week, 10, 1, 18.

Smith, Carl B. (Ed.) (1991) Alternative Assessment of Performance in the Language Arts. Bloomington, Indiana: ERIC & Phi Delta Kappan.

Stenmark, J.K. (1991). Math portfolios: A New Form of Assessment. Teaching K-8, (5), 62-64.

Tierney, R.J., Carter, M.A. & Desai, L.E. (1991). Portfolio Assessment in the Reading-Writing Classroom. Norwood, MA: Christopher-Gordon Publishers.

Valencia, S. (1990). A portfolio approach to classroom reading assessment: The whys, whats, and hows. The Reading Teacher, 42(1), 338-340.

Vavrus, L. (1990). Put portfolios to the test. Instructor, 100, 48-53.

Vermont Department of Education. (1990). Vermont's Assessment Program. Montpelier, Vermont: Vermont State Department of Education.

Wiggins, G. (1989). A true test: Toward more authentic and equitable assessment, Phi Delta Kappan, 708.

Wiggins, G. (1990). The Case for Authentic Assessment. (Washington, DC: ERIC Digest No. EDO TM 90 10)

Wolf, Robert L. (1975). Trial by jury: A new evaluation method, Phi Delta Kappan, 57(3), 185-187.

Wolf, D.P. (1989). Portfolio assessment: Sampling student work. Educational Leadership. 46(7), 35-39.

Worthen, B.R. & Spandel, V. (1991). Putting the Standardized Test Debate in Perspective. Educational Leadership , 48(2), 65-69.